note counts

The Schools' Instrumental
Music Service in the 1990s

Caroline Sharp

Published in 1991
by the National Foundation for Educational Research,
The Mere, Upton Park, Slough, Berkshire SL1 2DQ

ISBN 0 7005 1303 5

The National Foundation for Educational Research

The National Foundation for Educational Research in England and Wales (NFER) was founded in 1946 and is Britain's leading educational research institution. NFER's main role is to carry out research and development projects in all sectors of the public educational system and in professional and vocational training.

NFER is an independent organisation. As such, its approach is scientific, apolitical and non-partisan. The expert and experienced staff of the Foundation make use of a wide range of modern research techniques in their work. By means of surveys, interviews and case studies, NFER has provided objective evidence for a variety of audiences such as teachers; LEA advisers/inspectors; teacher educators; professional artists and parents. In addition to projects determined by its members, it undertakes a large number of sponsored projects at the request of government departments, local authorities and individual professional organisations.

The Author

Caroline Sharp has a degree in Sociology from the University of Leicester. She is a Senior Research Officer at the NFER, and has worked there for nine years. Her previous research experience encompasses a wide range of topics including studies on early childhood education, assessment methods for lower attaining students and an evaluation of the Enterprise in Higher Education (EHE) initiative.

Caroline has pursued her interest in arts education through a number of research studies, such as a survey of the arts component in initial training for primary teachers; case studies of good practice in teacher education for the arts; a conference report on performing arts courses for students post-16; and a study of the work of professional artists in schools.

Contents

Acknowledgements

I welcome this opportunity to express my gratitude to the people who helped make this research possible. I wish to thank the sponsors of this research and their representatives: the NFER Management Board; Kenneth Baird of the Arts Council of Great Britain; and Simon Richey of the Calouste Gulbenkian Foundation.

I am most grateful for the practical support provided by the UK Council for Music Education and Training and to their Secretary, Linda Cummins, for her good humoured and efficient replies to my requests for information.

The research would not have succeeded without the responses of music advisers, inspectors and heads of service to the questionnaire. I know that the questions took considerable time to answer and that some respondents went to the trouble of compiling figures especially for this study; all at an extremely busy time of year.

I am particularly grateful to the advisers, inspectors, school staff and consultants who gave up their valuable time to be interviewed and made very useful comments on the descriptions of their current practice which appear in the report.

I would also like to extend a special word of thanks to Shirley Cleave for her comments on the draft questionnaire and on the report; and to Karen Dust (Eastern Arts Board), Elizabeth Poulson (ISM), Maurice Jennings (Musicians' Union), Alan Vincent (MANA) and John Stephens (Trinity College of Music) for their advice, help and support throughout the research.

I am grateful to Lara Carim, Margaret Hitchcock and Megan Weindling for their assistance in extracting information from the 108 questionnaires. I would also like to thank Lesley Kendal (Senior Statistician at NFER) for her help with statistical analyses and her comments on the draft report.

Other colleagues at NFER deserve a special mention: Judy Bradley for her guidance of the research and Felicity Fletcher-Campbell for her helpful comments on the draft report. I am most grateful to Pauline Pearce, Jane Westing, Iris Ashby, Moci Carter and Maura Stock for their patience, good humour and excellent secretarial work; and to Enver Carim (Publications Manager and Press Officer), Tim Wright (Graphics Officer) and Mary Hargreaves (Media Resources Officer) for their contribution to the design and publication of this report.

Foreword by **John Stephens**

We all experience change with a mixture of apprehension and excitement. The unfolding development of ideas in a carefully crafted musical composition; the recognition of increased skill and understanding in a student's performance; an advance in technology which opens new opportunities and challenges to existing practice: all confront us in different ways, to meet and to accept change. Some find it easier than others to cope with change. "Where will it all lead?" some will ask. Change is about living, and living is about change.

This is true of the structures and patterns which have evolved in the delivery of music education in our schools, and in particular, of instrumental tuition. We operate within a framework which provides a security, and any changes can be viewed as either an opportunity or a threat. Our perceptions are influenced by where we are and what role we play in this operation.

As parents we will want the best for our child, with opportunities for the development of their potential for performing and playing with others, and gaining satisfaction from being involved in worthwhile musical experiences. As pupils we will seek to extend our interests, explore, enjoy and achieve the best musical results of which we are capable. As teachers we will thrive on the satisfaction of watching our pupils develop skills, confidence and understanding in their performances. As policy-makers we will interpret needs, determine priorities and exert influence to ensure an effective service.

Our perspective on changes within the instrumental music service is influenced by what we perceive to be happening around us, our immediate colleagues, nearby authorities and by what we read and hear in the media. For sensible strategic planning at local and national levels we need a basis of factual information. The research undertaken for the production of this volume provides such a platform. Woven into the statistical detail are the views and perspectives of many who have helped to influence and shape the present structures for the instrumental music services. If some have resonances of concern for the future it is likely to stem from their professional dedication.

For policy-makers, teachers, parents, and even some pupils, it provides a basis for considering the achievements of the past and the possibilities for the future. In the inevitable future changes in the instrumental teaching service it is the pupils who must not be 'short-changed'.

John Stephens is currently Head of the Music Education Department at Trinity College of Music and was formerly Staff Inspector for Music and HMI (Her Majesty's Inspector of Schools). He was Vice Chairman of the National Curriculum Music Working Group.

Executive Summary

Introduction

In February 1991 the National Foundation for Educational Research (NFER) began a five-month study of the nature and role of instrumental music provision in England and Wales. The main focus of the study was to discover how recent changes in funding and in education as a whole were affecting this non-statutory service. The research was funded by the NFER, with financial assistance from the Arts Council of Great Britain and the Calouste Gulbenkian Foundation. The study also received practical support from the UK Council for Music Education and Training (UKCMET).

Research methods

The research used two main methods of data collection: a questionnaire survey sent to the music adviser/inspector or head of instrumental music service in all 120 Local Education Authorities (LEAs) in England and Wales; and a series of interviews with representatives from music organisations, and with LEA and school staff in a small number of authorities. The survey was sent out in May, and responses were received from 108 (90 per cent) of authorities.

The recent context

The provisions of the 1988 Education Reform Act included three elements of particular significance to instrumental music services : legislation regarding charging for school activities; the introduction of Local Management of Schools (LMS); and a framework for a National Curriculum, including music as one of ten subjects to be taught in all maintained primary and secondary schools.

Recently, concern has begun to mount about the funding position of some instrumental music services, particularly those in areas facing the threat or imposition of community charge capping. Some music educators, parents and musicians have expressed the fear that children may be denied the chance to learn to play a musical instrument in future. This is because, in some areas, local authorities, schools and parents would be unable or unwilling to pay for this service.

The contribution of the Instrumental Music Services

The instrumental music services offer support to children wishing to learn to play a musical instrument. They also provide resources to schools such as the supply of musical instruments, performances by staff ensembles, advice and in-service training for teachers. With the introduction of National Curriculum music for children aged 5 to 14 in Autumn 1992, it is likely that the supportive role of the services will expand, in order to help school-based staff implement the new curriculum.

In addition to their work in schools, most LEA services have music centres which offer a range of activities to children and, in some cases, provide resources for the wider community. These centres also represent a focus for the many youth ensembles, bands, choirs and orchestras which perform in their local communities and have a national and international reputation for musical excellence.

The music services also provide an early training ground for some children who will become the professional musicians and music teachers of the future.

A period of change

This research has shown that instrumental music services are experiencing a period of rapid change. There appears to be an increasing disparity in the financial position of services in different areas, and some respondents predicted that the effects of charging policies and of Local Management of Schools will cause increased disparity of provision within LEAs in future. This was because schools and parents in affluent areas would be willing and able to pay for tuition whereas schools in 'deprived' areas may have other priorities for the use of delegated funds, and parents may be discouraged from asking for tuition for their children where charges are levied.

Changes in funding

Over a third of respondents to the survey said they had experienced change in the funding of their services between 1989/90 and 1990/91. In thirty-four per cent of LEAs, changes had resulted in cuts in funding for instrumental music. The most commonly reported cause of these cuts was the imposition, or threat, of community charge capping. There was a similar degree of change from 1990/ 91 to 1991/92, when 38 per cent of respondents reported budget cuts. Twenty-one LEAs had suffered budget cuts in both years; and two LEA services were closed entirely, one in 1990 and one in 1991. On average, the areas most hit by financial cuts were the metropolitan districts and the (outer) London boroughs.

The most common result of budget cuts was a reduction in staffing. The information from 82 LEAs showed an overall loss of 129.2 full-time equivalent (FTE) posts, a drop of five per cent between 1989/90 and 1991/92. There were considerable differences between areas, with metropolitan districts reporting the greatest staffing losses, amounting to an average decrease of 15 per cent over three years. On the other hand, some LEAs reported funding and staffing gains. Eleven LEAs reported a funding increase in 1990/91 and at the time of the survey, six respondents knew that they would receive an increase in 1991/92. These funding increases were caused by a number of factors including increases in LEA funding, parental contributions and additional revenue from schools. Funding increases were most common in English counties, and this was reflected in a much lower level of staffing decreases reported for these authorities from 1989/90 to 1991/92, despite the loss of 40 FTE posts in one English county. In another county, a music trust had recruited 16 FTE new staff in the same period. The estimated total number of FTE staff in England and Wales in 1991/92 was approximately 3,500, the same number as estimated for 1985/86 in a previous NFER study (Cleave, S. and Dust, K.1989).

Responses to a period of change

The survey results revealed that the nature and extent of instrumental provision was changing, in response to legislative and funding forces.

The effect of **LMS** was apparent in a number of survey results. For example, over half of respondents stated that the main purpose of their service was to provide a high quality service to schools. This type of response was not evident in the previous NFER research study, conducted five years previously (Cleave, S. and Dust, K. 1989). A substantial minority of respondents said that tuition was allocated to schools on the basis of the LMS formula, related to the number of pupils in a school. Others will be moving towards this system in future. Comparisons with earlier studies showed an increase in provision to primary schools.

The legislation regarding **charging for school activities** had affected instrumental services in a variety of ways. For example, just under a third of LEAs had introduced (or re-introduced) charges for tuition following the implementation of the 'charging' legislation. The survey revealed some confusion over the definition of 'individual' tuition (which can be subject to a charge). Some service providers were charging parents for tuition taking place in small groups, on the basis that each child received individual attention within the group. Others had moved from group to individual tuition, so that charges could be made.

Despite these effects, over half of the respondents said that the charging legislation had not affected instrumental tuition in their authorities.

The introduction of **National Curriculum music** was reflected by the fact that over half the instrumental services were adopting strategies to further the relationship between instrumental tuition and music education in schools. Strategies included: general support for classroom music activities; in-service training for school staff; staffing policies (for example, the creation of special posts of responsibility); and performances, workshops and special projects. On the other hand, over a third of respondents felt that a closer integration between the service and class music teaching was either problematic or undesirable. The main concern was the perceived tension between their ability to offer a specialised service and adopting a more generalist, supportive role, given the current level of funding.

The level of provision

Based on responses to the survey, we would estimate that about 467,500 pupils were receiving instrumental music tuition in 1990/91. This represents between six and seven per cent of the total school population in England and Wales. The equivalent estimate for the number of **schools** receiving regular visits from instrumental service staff in 1990/91 was 17,000 (64 per cent). Provision was highest for secondary schools (around 97 per cent). Approximately 63 per cent of primary schools were visited by instrumental staff, and only 16 per cent of special schools.

Despite the fact that the estimated total number of instrumental staff employed in 1985/86 and 1991/92 was the same, provision in 1990/1 (in terms of the number of schools and pupils reached) was somewhat higher than that in 1985/86. This apparent contradiction is explained, in part, by a recent increase in the size of tuition groups in about a third of LEAs.

The research also revealed a change in the type of instrumental tuition offered. Although the main orchestral instruments (strings, brass and woodwind) dominated, there was a slight decrease in the number of LEAs offering tuition for these instruments. The main increases since the 1986 NFER study were apparent for modern instruments (electric/bass guitar, electric keyboards) and for instruments outside the Western tradition (steel pans, sitar, tabla and harmonium).

Music Trusts, Agencies and Foundations

Semi-autonomous agencies, trusts and foundations represented an attractive alternative to music services for some LEAs. The survey revealed that these types of organisations already existed in four LEAs, were being set up in seven, and were under active consideration in a further ten. The main reason for the increasing popularity of these alternatives to an LEA service was that they were perceived to be less vulnerable to cuts in local government expenditure. Also, as a third party, an agency, trust or foundation may levy charges for tuition in circumstances where a service may not. However, some participants in the research expressed the view that these alternatives would not necessarily be viable in 'socially deprived' areas of England and Wales.

Future challenges

Respondents predicted increasing uncertainty for their services in future, arising mainly from the delegation of centrally-held LEA funding to schools. Some could foresee expansion, with increased income from schools' delegated budgets and parents. On the other hand, just under a third of respondents predicted that negative effects on their services would result from LMS. These fears included: an uneven spread of provision, with rural schools and those in 'deprived' areas losing out; fragmentation of provision; a depletion of the overall instrumental music budget and even the complete closure of the service. Other factors causing concern included an increasing difficulty in timetabling lessons, the effects on LEA budgets of schools opting out of LEA control, and uncertainty over the future of local government.

An overview of the findings

Taken overall, these findings suggest that there has been an increase in instrumental service staff and provision after 1986 (the time of the previous NFER survey) but that this has been followed by a more recent decline, particularly in the number of staff employed. The most common reason given for cuts in staffing was the imposition, or threat, of community charge capping (which had contributed to the closure of the entire service in two authorities). Different effects were being felt in different areas. Although many services (particularly those in metropolitan districts and London boroughs) had experienced cuts in funding, others (particularly those in English counties) had expanded. Many respondents were concerned about their future funding position, and some predicted further closures of services if LEAs decide to delegate the money for instrumental music services to schools in future.

A possible way forward

Some participants in the research suggested that instrumental services should receive a central government grant. Such a system was believed to have a number of advantages, because it would ensure a basic level of instrumental provision in all areas, while enabling service managers to develop their existing provision to meet the need for classroom music support. In a time of such insecurity, a national funding system would help to ensure that, in all areas of England and Wales 'the music will play on'.

1 Introduction

This report presents the findings of an NFER research project carried out in 1991. The research investigated the nature and role of instrumental music services in England and Wales. At the time, there was growing concern among music educators, service providers, parents and musicians, that cuts to music service budgets would result in a loss of access to instrumental music tuition for many children.

What do instrumental music services do?

Instrumental music provision can seem a somewhat 'hidden' service. Typically the service is delivered by peripatetic tutors who visit schools and teach small groups of children who are withdrawn from their normal school lessons. Many children also attend music centres, but their lessons generally take place after school hours and the fact that they do so is often only apparent to their parents, their music tutor, and the children themselves. Tuition provided by the service is a scarce resource, reaching only a minority of children. Its most 'public' face is the youth bands, choirs and orchestras which are a feature of most LEAs. Although instrumental music services fulfil a number of roles, the fostering of musical talent and the general concentration on a Western classical repertoire have laid them open to charges of elitism. What, then, is the real contribution of these (non-statutory) music services to the education of children?

Figure 1 illustrates some of the ways in which the instrumental service contributes to the work of primary and secondary schools, to the education of individual children and to the enhancement of the cultural life of the wider community.

Figure 1 The role of the instrumental music service

YOUTH BANDS, ORCHESTRAS AND CHOIRS

- Opportunities for young people to develop their social, musical and performance skills
- Contributing to the musical life of the community
- Performing nationally and internationally
- Preparation for a career in music

PRIMARY SCHOOLS

- Tuition for individual pupils
- Workshops for classes and teachers
- Performances by instrumental music staff ensembles
- Support for class music
- Contributing to the musical life of the school

LEA INSTRUMENTAL MUSIC SERVICE, TRUST OR AGENCY

MUSIC CENTRES

- Opportunities for group music-making
- Advanced tuition for individuals and groups
- Instruments, music libraries and facilities for practice
- Specialist music courses
- Provision for young children, parents and other adults
- Social enjoyment and interest

SECONDARY SCHOOLS

- Tuition for individual pupils, including advanced work for GCSE and 'A' level students
- INSET for school staff
- Performances by instrumental staff ensembles
- Support for class music
- Contributing to the musical life of the school

SPECIAL PROVISION

- Tuition for 'non-Western' music and for children with special educational needs

Work in schools

A research study of parents' views on their children's musical education in the primary school (Addison, 1990) revealed a considerable level of parental support for children being given the opportunity to learn to play an orchestral or band instrument at school. The survey, which was carried out in nine schools located in inner city and rural areas of Northumberland, received responses from 1,119 parents (about 56 per cent of the possible total of parents in those schools). The survey revealed strong support for three items in particular: the teaching of singing (94 per cent); giving children opportunities to listen to music (91 per cent); and opportunities to learn an orchestral/band instrument (91 per cent). In addition, the author was somewhat surprised to find that a majority of the 21 per cent of parents who claimed no interest in music themselves would nevertheless like their children to have the opportunity to learn to play an instrument at school.

As far as provision of instrumental tuition in schools is concerned, a recent HMI publication, which was based on inspections of some 285 primary schools between 1982 and 1989, stated that:

> *Approximately one-third of the schools had some kind of support from peripatetic instrumental teachers, who sometimes introduced all children, including those receiving instrumental tuition, to a wider range of musical experiences.*
> (GB, DES, 1991a)

This statement identifies two potential roles for instrumental services: the tuition of small groups of children, and a broader contribution to the music curriculum as a whole.

In Autumn 1992 a national music curriculum for children aged 5 to 14 will be introduced. The final report of the Music Working Group (GB, DES 1991b) states that, in order to fulfil their proposals: 'pupils will need to play instruments as well as sing'. The authors go on to say:

By key stage 2, pupils should be exercising their skills on a wider range of instruments requiring more sophisticated technical skills. It will be important for pupils to have experiences which lay secure technical foundations in playing an instrument. The need for specialist instrumental tuition becomes apparent at this stage and continues for those pupils with the interest and commitment to continue with instrumental study - throughout their schooling.

The report also points out that specific techniques are rarely transferable between instruments. The implication of this is that children may need tuition from more than one specialist teacher in order to develop skills in playing more than one instrument and that teachers should not be expected to teach too wide a range of instruments, although they often teach a range of instruments within a group (woodwind, brass, etc).

In relation to the contribution of instrumental services to the general music curriculum, the report points out that 'many instrumental teachers have developed strategies for group and ensemble tuition, and are closely relating their approaches to those used in class lessons'. It calls upon each school to have within its general policy a clear statement on its provision for instrumental teaching, and advises heads and governors that: 'Such a statement should define the relationship between instrumental and vocal tuition and class music provision.'(GB, DES 1991b).

Another important aspect of musical experience within schools, identified in both the HMI document and the Music Working Group report, is the opportunity for children to experience live music. Instrumental services have many talented musicians on their staff, some of whom have formed ensembles and bands which give performances in schools. In addition some instrumental services also provide resources to schools such as musical instruments and equipment, help with school productions (for example, with performances for parents) and contribute to in-service training for primary and secondary teachers. A number of such services make provision for children with special educational needs and contribute towards multi-cultural education by providing tuition on instruments for the performance of music outside the Western tradition.

Music centre activities

Most authorities have music centres which provide opportunities for children to extend the musical experiences they have in school. Music centres enable children from a number of schools to meet and work together in groups and ensembles. Many music centres offer a wide range of music courses to help children at different stages of musical development to build up their skills and widen their range of experience in playing different types of instrument. Some enable children to work creatively on projects combining music with other performing arts. In a number of LEAs, the music centres act as a focus for community music-making, offering classes for pre-school age children and adults, and providing the local community with access to resources such as soundproofed practice rooms, recording equipment, instruments and music libraries.

Youth bands, orchestras and choirs

Music centres also provide the focus for the formation of youth orchestras, bands and choirs. Most authorities have at least one such ensemble and they contribute in a variety of ways to the cultural life of their communities. As Baroness David said during a recent House of Lords debate: 'In percentage of population Britain has more young people's orchestras, ensembles, bands and choirs than any other European country and certainly rivals the United States.' (*Hansard*, 13th February 1991.) The quality of these youth orchestras and choirs is high and many of them contribute towards the annual schools' promenade concerts and the National Festival of Music for Youth. Many also undertake concert tours in other countries, acting in a sense as cultural ambassadors for their country. As one of the music advisers who contributed to this research pointed out: 'British youth orchestras are the envy of Europe and give so many young musicians such fulfilling and rewarding experiences, as well as greater ties with other countries.'

Professional preparation

In addition to the personal interest and pleasure that learning to play an instrument can bring, a small number of children who learn to play an instrument or to sing with the support of tuition from instrumental services, will eventually go on to make a professional career in music. Although there has been no national research on this relationship, two small-scale investigations (Mills, S. 1985; ABO, 1991) suggest that a high proportion of the professional musicians in this country have received instrumental tuition from an LEA service.

In 1982, a research study of professional musicians in three symphony orchestras showed that, of the 46 musicians who responded to a questionnaire, 22 had taken up their principal instrument due to the influence of an educational institution (Mills, J. 1985). More recently, a 'straw' poll of the members of 10 professional orchestras revealed that half or more of the players who responded had received free instrumental teaching at some point during their school life, and the proportion was over two-thirds in seven of the orchestras (Association of British Orchestras, 1991). In response to the poll, 19 members of the Bournemouth Sinfonietta added that they would not have become professional musicians without the influence of the tuition they had received from an LEA service. These studies serve to illustrate the role of the music service in identifying early musical potential and in helping lay the foundations of a musical career. For some stringed instruments, early identification and tuition is particularly important because, as the Music Working Group report argues, those wishing to pursue a career as string players need to begin learning to play at an early age.

It is also important to acknowledge the role of instrumental services in helping to prepare the music teachers of the future. There currently appears to be a shortage of music teachers at secondary level, and many primary teachers lack confidence in this area. With the introduction of National Curriculum music, it is likely that the demand for music teachers will increase.

Fears for the future of instrumental services: the recent context

In late 1989, a number of threats to the continued funding of instrumental music services were reported. A combination of factors was at work, not least the requirement for some local authorities to cut back their spending in order to keep their community charges at an acceptable level.

Concern for the future of instrumental music services prompted the formation of a new pressure group 'Save Instrumental Teaching!' (SIT!) which organised a national conference in January 1991, and called for 'immediate steps' to be taken by the Government to protect the funding of LEA music services.

Press reports with headlines such as 'Music at risk of playing second fiddle' (*The Independent*) and 'Cuts policies meet chorus of disapproval' (*Times Educational Supplement*) began to appear.

In February 1991, the House of Lords debated the threats posed to instrumental music services by community charge capping and the Local Management of Schools. Lord Donaldson of Kingsbridge drew on personal experience to describe the many advantages of instrumental music tuition. He went on to say, 'It cannot be right to let such a fruitful series of combined efforts run down and slowly wither away. It looks very much as if that is what is being allowed to happen.' Speaking on behalf of the Government, Baroness Blatch (Parliamentary Under-Secretary of State for the Department of the Environment) replied:

> *On the evidence we have so far, I do not believe that fear to be justified .... It is too soon to reach firm conclusions, since the picture we have at this stage is a confused one .... My expectation is that after a period of uncertainty while new arrangements are worked out, we shall see a better organised and better publicised service emerge in many areas than has existed in the past. (Hansard, 13th February 1991.)*

However, fears for the fate of music services continued to mount, and in March the Musicians' Union published a list of 29 local authorities where music services were faced with the threat of cuts, mainly attributed to the 'capping' of community charge levels by central government.

In July of the same year, the National Festival of Music for Youth organised its annual music event at the Royal Festival Hall. To draw attention to threatened cuts, the organisers held a 'Keep Music Alive in Our Schools Day'. Simon Rattle conducted around 2,000 young musicians in a specially commissioned piece by Howard Blake. The music was entitled 'Let Music Live'. Nicola Loud, who had won the award of BBC Young Musician of the Year, led the orchestra. She recalled the importance of her early music tuition which had begun in the primary school.

The Music for Youth Festival attracted a great deal of press attention. On the morning of the performance of 'Let Music Live', Mr. Tim Eggar, junior Education Minister, was interviewed on the BBC Radio 4 programme 'Today'. In response to a question about the reported cuts in music services, he said: 'Music provision is in a stage of transition. As Local Management of Schools comes in, more budgets are devolved down to schools and therefore the choice rests increasingly with schools. Obviously the nature of music provision is going to change.'

It was in this context that the research was carried out. While many people were concerned about the future of instrumental music services, there existed no independent research information on the nature and extent of change, and on the response of music services to the influences of the 1988 Education Reform Act.

Background to this research

The research was undertaken with three main aims in mind:

i)   to build on the results of previous NFER research in order to document national trends in instrumental music provision;

ii)   to examine the implications of a range of strategies adopted by LEAs and schools to provide or retain instrumental tuition following the provisions of the Education Reform Act;

iii) to consider the changing role of instrumental services in supporting the introduction of music as a foundation subject in the National Curriculum.

The research was funded by the membership programme of the NFER, which undertakes a number of small research studies of potential value and interest to its members, principally Local Education Authorities. The research was supported by the UK Council for Music Education and Training (UKCMET) and was assisted by grants from the Arts Council of Great Britain and the Calouste Gulbenkian Foundation.

The research design

The research began in February 1991 and took five months to complete. It used two main methods to gather information: a national questionnaire survey sent to the music adviser/inspector or head of music service in each English and Welsh LEA; and interviews with representatives from music organisations, and LEA and school staff in a small number of authorities.

The survey took place during the summer term of 1991. The timing was not ideal, as it coincided with one of the busiest times of the year for LEAs. However, it did enable questions about the following school year to be answered with some degree of certainty by most respondents.

The questionnaire was sent to all 120 LEAs in England and Wales, including the small island authorities of Man, Scilly, Guernsey and Jersey. A very high response rate was eventually achieved, as can be seen in Table 1.1, which also gives a breakdown of the responses obtained from different types of authority.

Table 1.1:   LEAs taking part in the survey

LEAs	No. in England and Wales	No. responding	%
English counties	39	35	90
Metropolitan districts	36	31	86
London boroughs	20	18	90
Inner London authorities	13	12	92
Islands	4	4	100
Wales	8	8	100
Total	120	108	90

As the table shows, an overall response of 90 per cent was achieved, and the proportion of responses from each type of authority was high. In addition, an Assistant Education Officer from an inner London authority replied by letter, saying that instrumental tuition in his authority's one school was provided by a neighbouring LEA. Another response, from a London borough, was received too late to be included in the analysis. The high response to the questionnaire enabled a fairly representative picture of the national changes affecting instrumental tuition to be compiled.

Analysis of the survey data was carried out and in some cases comparisons were made with information collected in a previous NFER study, which had involved a survey of LEAs conducted five years previously. The earlier research was carried out by two researchers over a period of two years. The findings of that research were published in a report entitled *A Sound Start* (Cleave, S. and Dust, K., 1989).

The earlier report contained a detailed account of the extent of music tuition offered by peripatetic staff in schools and music centres. The 1991 research questionnaire contained several questions which were comparable with those in the previous study. This has enabled the new research to document changes and to identify trends over time. However, it should be noted that, although both surveys achieved high responses, small differences in the results from the two pieces of research may be due to differences in the composition of the samples, rather than to changes over time. The two surveys did not receive responses from exactly the same authorities. In particular, it should be noted that when the first survey took place in 1986, inner London was under the control of the Inner London Education Authority (ILEA). By 1991, 13 new inner London authorities had been formed, 12 of which responded to the second survey.

The outline of the report

This report is divided into six chapters, each of which focuses on a particular aspect of the instrumental service provided in England and Wales.

Chapter 1 has provided some background to the study and has outlined the research design. In **Chapter 2**, the issue of change is addressed. The chapter presents evidence on changes in the funding for instrumental music and looks at the consequences of such changes for the number of instrumental teachers employed. **Chapter 3** focuses on the provision of instrumental tuition in schools and music centres. It considers the role of the service and the number of children and schools currently receiving tuition. The selection of schools and pupils to receive the service is addressed. The chapter also looks at trends in the tuition of a number of instruments (including voice) and identifies who is responsible for purchasing and maintaining musical instruments.

In **Chapter 4**, certain aspects of the management of instrumental services are addressed, including the management structure, quality control and the conditions of employment of instrumental staff. **Chapter 5** contains an in-depth assessment of the major current and future challenges to instrumental music services in England and Wales, arising from the 1988 Education Reform Act. Three main issues are addressed in detail: charging for instrumental tuition; the delegation of LEA funds to schools; and the introduction of a National Curriculum for music. The chapter ends by outlining a possible funding scenario which some music educators believe would ensure an equitable distribution of resources for instrumental tuition in the future.

Chapter 6 focuses on different forms of organisation of music services, such as agencies, trusts and foundations. Information from the survey is used to identify how many LEAs are considering setting up such organisations. This is followed by interview material used to construct portrayals of the service offered in four authorities and in inner London. The chapter ends with a summary of the main constraints and opportunities affecting the operation of music trusts, agencies and foundations.

The report concludes with a short section drawing out some of the main findings and suggesting some points which service managers and LEA advisers/inspectors may wish to consider when considering the future role and operation of their instrumental music services.

2 Funding for Instrumental Music Services

Introduction

This chapter addresses some important issues concerning the funding of instrumental music in England and Wales. The chapter begins by outlining the main sources of financial support for instrumental tuition and for music centres, choirs and orchestras. It also considers whether the proportions of funding contributed by different 'partners' have changed in the past five years.

The chapter then presents evidence on past and future changes in the total amount of funding received. It identifies the main causes of such changes and their effects on the provision of instrumental music.

A third section in the chapter focuses on staffing levels for different groups of instruments and for vocal tuition, comparing staffing levels over a three-year period. A final section summarises the main changes in proportions and levels of funding and in staffing for instrumental music in England and Wales.

Who funds instrumental music?

A few years ago, the answer to this question was relatively clear and unambiguous: by far the greatest funding source for instrumental music was local authority expenditure, usually from the education budget. There were, of course, some additional sources of funding such as parental fees and a limited amount of sponsorship. An article in the *Daily Telegraph* (Izbicki, 1981) estimated that about half the LEAs in the country were charging parents for some aspects of instrumental teaching. Following a court case in 1981, which ruled that such charges were illegal for activities comprising part of the curriculum or taking place during school time, many LEAs changed their policy. In 1986, the NFER survey of instrumental music revealed that about a third of LEAs charged for lessons at their music centres but only five LEAs requested voluntary contributions from parents towards the cost of instrumental tuition in schools. (The effects of the 'charging' legislation on instrumental tuition are discussed in Chapter 5.) Some music services were able to raise small amounts of money from other sources such as instrument hire, fees for courses and box office returns from concerts.

The 1991 NFER survey asked respondents to indicate which of the four possible contributors (LEAs, schools, parents and 'other') were the main funding source(s) for i) instrumental tuition and ii) music centres, youth choirs and orchestras. The survey results are shown in Tables 2.1 and 2.2 below.

Funding for instrumental tuition

Table 2.1   Main sources of funding for instrumental tuition in 1990/91 (108 LEAs)

Funding sources	N	%
LEA only	68	63
LEA and parents	18	16
LEA and schools	9	8
LEA, schools and parents	4	4
schools only	3	3
schools and parents	2	2
parents only	2	2
other*	2	2
Total	108	100

*   (LEA, parents, box office returns and sponsorship; parents and grants from a charitable trust.)

Table 2.1 shows that, in the majority of cases, the LEA is still the sole reported funding source for instrumental tuition. However, there is a substantial change from the position for the school year 1985/86, towards more plural funding, involving schools and parents. Of the 108 LEAs responding, LEA funds contributed to instrumental tuition in 100 (93 per cent); parents contributed in 28 (26 per cent) and schools in 18 (17 per cent). Where tuition was funded from more than one source, respondents were asked to give the relative proportions of funding contributed by each. This revealed that, in the 32 cases where the LEA contributed alongside schools and/or parents, the LEA was generally responsible for the larger proportion of total funding, or shared the funding equally with parents or schools (only six respondents reported that the LEA contributed less than 50 per cent of the instrumental budget in their areas).

The findings also reveal that parents were the sole contributing body in two LEAs. In one case (a metropolitan district) the LEA had recently ceased funding instrumental provision altogether and parents were therefore the only remaining source of funding for instrumental tuition. In the other (a London borough) the LEA granted licences to instrumental teachers who could then work in schools. Individual instrumental lessons were arranged by schools but paid for by parents.

Funding for music centres, youth choirs and orchestras

Table 2.2   Main sources of funding for music centres, youth choirs and orchestras in 1990/91 (104 LEAs)

Funding Sources	N	%
LEA only	52	50
LEA and parents	29	28
LEA and fundraising*	6	5
LEA, parents and fundraising	5	5
parents and fundraising	5	5
LEA and schools	4	4
parents only	2	2
LEA, parents and schools	1	1
Total	104	100

* (The category of 'fundraising' includes box office income, donations from charities, commercial sponsorship and support organisations.)

Table 2.2 shows the main sources of funding for music centres, youth orchestras and choirs, identified by 104 LEAs. Three LEAs were unable to supply this information and one (a small island authority) had no music centre, choir or orchestra.

The table shows that 50 per cent of the 104 LEAs were solely responsible for funding these items. When mixed funding is taken into account, LEA funds were contributing in 97 (93 per cent) of authorities, parents in 42 (40 per cent), fundraising in 16 (15 per cent) and schools in five (five per cent).

There were 45 authorities where the LEA was a funding partner. Of these, the majority received most of their funding from the LEA (only three respondents reported that their LEA was a minority funding partner). Parents were the sole contributors in two LEAs (one London borough, and one metropolitan district). Both reported that their music centres offered a fairly restricted range of activities.

As well as contributing funds in the form of tuition fees, parents were also reported to be contributing through fundraising. Many youth choirs and orchestras have 'friends' organisations whose membership is drawn predominantly from parents. These support groups are generally responsible for raising funds for the young musicians through such activities as fêtes and jumble sales, personal donations and for attracting money from other sponsors. Fundraising, sponsorship and box office returns contributed towards the cost of music centres, youth choirs and orchestras in 16 (15 per cent) of LEAs.

Changes in proportions of funding

The questionnaire asked if there had been any change in the overall proportions of funding for tuition, music centres, youth choirs and orchestras in the past five years. Almost three-quarters of the (104) respondents who answered this question said there had been no such change. Of the 28 (27 per cent) who reported a change, 24 gave further details. In 21 (19 per cent) LEAs, the reported change was that LEAs were now contributing a lower proportion of the funding, resulting in a higher proportion being found from parents (in 17 LEAs) and delegated school budgets (in four LEAs). Other changes reported by three LEAs were a decrease in school contributions in relation to contributions from parents; and unusually, an increase in LEA funding in relation to parental contributions in two cases.

Increases and decreases in funding

Respondents were asked to indicate any changes in the overall level of funding (for tuition, music centres, orchestras and choirs) in 1990/91, 1991/92 and any known changes in the next five years.

Changes from 1989/90 to 1990/91

Figure 2.1 shows reported changes in overall funding (allowing for inflation) for instrumental tuition, music centres etc between the previous school year (1989/90) and 1990/91, the year of the survey. The figure shows a breakdown of responses by type of authority.

Over half of the respondents reported no change between the two years. However, a substantial minority (44 per cent) said that there had been changes, and 34 per cent reported a decrease in funding for these items.

Figure 2.1   Changes from 1989/90 to 1990/91 in the overall level of funding for instrumental tuition, music centres, youth choirs and orchestras, allowing for inflation (106 LEAs)

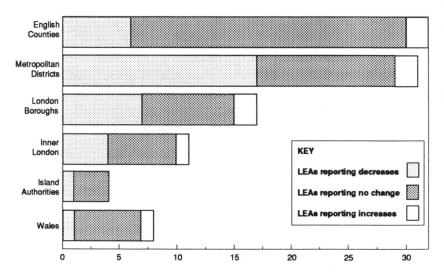

The figure shows that over half the respondents from metropolitan districts (17 out of 31) reported decreases. Decreases in funding were also reported by a fairly high proportion of London authorities: taking London boroughs and inner London authorities together, 11 out of 28 (almost 40 per cent) reported a decrease in funding for instrumental music services from 1989/90 to 1990/91.

An analysis of changes by geographical region showed that there was a 'cluster' of authorities in London and in the North of England (particularly Greater Manchester and West and South Yorkshire) reporting decreases in funding in 1990/91, compared with the previous year. There was no particular geographical pattern evident for authorities reporting increases in funding.

Respondents reporting changes in funding were asked to give further details of the causes and effects of the change.

Causes and effects of decreases in funding from 1989/90 to 1990/91

Thirty respondents gave information on the causes of cuts in instrumental music budgets. A majority of these respondents said that the cuts were due to a reduction in the education budget. In some cases this was, in turn, caused by reductions in local government spending due to community charge capping (or to measures taken by councils to avoid being capped). This factor had caused substantial cuts in 11 LEAs (six metropolitan districts, four counties and two London boroughs). Another cause of budget cuts for instrumental music identified in three LEAs (one metropolitan district and two London boroughs) was Local Management of Schools (LMS). LMS may cause decreases in funding because the funding decision rests with individual headteachers, some of whom may not decide to use funds delegated from the former instrumental service budget to purchase instrumental tuition. Two LEAs (one metropolitan district and one London borough) reported that their services were suffering from a combination of community charge capping and LMS.

Respondents reported that decreases in their budgets were having a variety of consequences, and most identified more than one type of effect. The main effects of financial reductions on instrumental music services were: cuts in staffing, reductions in expenditure on musical instruments and reduced provision of tuition in schools and music centres. Twenty LEAs reported staffing cuts. In some cases these were implemented by reducing the number of hours taught; in others they resulted in the loss of several teachers. Ten respondents reported that cuts had affected their stocks of musical instruments. Various strategies had been adopted such as freezing budgets for new purchases, cutting back on repairs or selling off the LEA's stocks of instruments. A few respondents reported that cuts had caused a reduction in the range of instruments taught. This had affected peripatetic services in two LEAs and music centre activities in three. One LEA reported the loss of its entire instrumental music service with effect from September 1990.

There were a number of other reported effects of budget cuts, including: a freeze in staff incentive allowances; cuts in the purchase of sheet music; difficulties in funding transport for young musicians; and in two cases where parents were charged for lessons, a reduction in the number of children receiving free tuition from remission schemes.

Causes and effects of increases in funding

Ten respondents provided information about the causes of funding increases for instrumental music in their authorities. Four of these respondents had received increases from their LEAs (two English counties, one metropolitan district and one Welsh LEA). In two other LEAs, the increase was due to additional revenue raised from parental contributions. Another LEA reported increased revenue from parental contributions and sponsorship. Two respondents from the London area said their funding was increased because schools were buying in additional instrumental tuition from their delegated budgets. In one metropolitan district, there was a small increase in funding due to sixth form reorganisation: a newly-formed tertiary college was now buying in instrumental tuition from the music service.

The funding increases had resulted in a variety of changes to instrumental provision, and several respondents reported more than one type of effect. The most commonly mentioned changes were: increased staffing (four LEAs); new/improved management structures, including incentive allowances (two LEAs); the formation of new orchestras and choirs (two LEAs); and the provision of tuition to a greater number of pupils (one LEA). One respondent commented that, although his LEA had increased funding recently, this had merely restored the music service to the position it had held ten years previously.

Changes from 1990/91 to 1991/92

The survey was carried out in the summer of 1991 when many LEA music inspectors/advisers and heads of music services already knew what their funding position would be in the following school year. However, sixteen respondents said they were unable to comment on changes from 1990/91 to 1991/92 because their budgets for the next year had not yet been finalised. The changes reported by the remaining 92 respondents are set out in Figure 2.2.

Figure 2.2   Changes from 1990/91 to 1991/92 in the overall level of funding for instrumental tuition, music centres, youth choirs and orchestras, allowing for inflation (92 LEAs)*

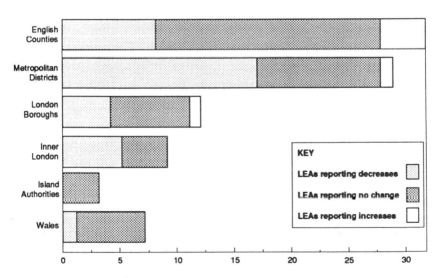

*   Sixteen respondents said they were unable to comment because funding decisions had not been finalised for 1991/92.

Figure 2.2 shows a pattern of reported changes similar to that in Figure 2.1. Over half of the respondents said there would be no change in their budgets next year. A substantial minority (45 per cent) reported budget changes, and most of these were decreases. The number of LEAs predicting increases for the following school year had fallen slightly when compared with the figures for 1989/90 to 1990/91. Only 6 LEAs (7 per cent) knew of an increase in funding in 1991/92, compared with 11 (10 per cent) the previous year. The number of LEAs predicting decreases remained about the same, but this represented a higher percentage of the total, because fewer LEAs had responded to this question.

Again, it was respondents from the metropolitan districts who reported the greatest proportion of reductions (17 out of 29 LEAs). There was also a high proportion of respondents from London LEAs reporting budget cuts (nine out of a total of 21 LEAs). In terms of geographical location, there was, again, a cluster of LEAs in London and the North of England reporting decreases in budgets for the following school year (1991/92).

The fact that the pattern of reported cuts was similar for the two years (1990/91 and 1991/92) would seem to suggest that some LEAs had sustained decreases in their budgets for two years running. In fact, 21 respondents reported two years of budget cuts, 13 of whom were in metropolitan districts. Three LEAs (two counties and one metropolitan district) reported two years of budget increases.

Causes and effects of decreases in funding from 1990/91 to 1991/92

The reported causes of change in overall funding and their predicted effects in 1991/92 followed a similar pattern to that reported for changes which had taken place in 1990/91.

Thirty-one respondents reported the causes of decreases in their budgets, the majority of which were due to cuts in the local authority education budget. Community charge capping was identified as the main factor in 12 LEAs (six of which were metropolitan districts). Two respondents predicted reductions due to LMS and another reported cuts due to a combination of community charge capping and LMS.

The predicted effects of these funding decreases were staffing cuts (including reduced incentive allowances and fewer full-time, permanent appointments), reduced provision to schools and pupils, a narrower range of instruments taught, fewer music centre activities, the loss of youth choirs and orchestras, old stocks of musical instruments not replaced, and the introduction of charges to parents. One LEA reported the loss of its entire instrumental service from September 1991 (the second closure of a music service since 1990).

Causes and effects of increases in funding from 1990/91 to 1991/92

Four respondents gave details of funding increases. These were caused by different combinations of factors in each case. One music service would receive an increase in its LEA grant. Another would receive a slight increase from the LEA (in order to help the service become an agency) and expected that it would attract additional revenue from schools' delegated budgets. It was predicted that increases in the number of parents paying for tuition would lead to expansion in two LEAs. In one of these LEAs, the music service had already been formed into a semi-autonomous music agency which received its income from schools. Some of the school headteachers were, in turn, asking parents to contribute towards the costs of tuition. (See Chapter 6 for more information on music trusts, agencies, and foundations.)

The main predicted effects of these funding increases were higher staffing levels and a greater spread of provision of tuition to schools and pupils. One county which had been granted a larger sum from the LEA would be able to reduce the fees charged to members of its area ensembles.

Changes in the next five years

The questionnaire asked respondents to report on any other known major changes in the source(s) and/or level of funding for instrumental music in the next five years.

Nearly half (44 per cent) of respondents identified major changes in their future funding position. Changes were reported in all types of LEA (13 counties, 14 Metropolitan districts, nine London boroughs, seven inner London authorities, four Welsh authorities, and one island). Respondents gave a variety of causes of change, but by far the greatest number (33 LEAs) reported that their budgets were likely to be affected (either positively or negatively) by the delegation of centrally held funds to schools under LMS.

Other changes which would affect instrumental music, identified by a minority of LEAs were: a reduction in the education budget due to schools opting out of local authority control (four LEAs), and predicted increases in parental charges (three LEAs). Several respondents also said that their LEA was considering setting up a semi-autonomous trust or agency to run music services in future. The impact of such changes on instrumental music is explored further in Chapters 5 and 6.

Changes in the numbers of instrumental teaching staff from 1989/90 to 1991/92

When changes occur in the funding of any service, one of the main areas to be affected is staffing. We wanted to know whether changes were occurring in the number of staff employed or the number of hours worked by instrumental teachers and instructors. We also wanted to find out whether such changes had had a differential impact on teachers of different 'families' of instruments.

The questionnaire asked for detailed information on the number of full-time equivalent (FTE) staff employed in three consecutive years. Respondents were also asked to specify the number of FTE teachers employed in different instrumental groups (including voice). This was obviously a time-consuming question for respondents to answer, particularly if their own staffing figures were not expressed in the same way as that requested in the question. It was a difficult question for respondents in inner London authorities to address, as many did not know the instrumental staffing position relating to their areas before the new authorities took over from the ILEA in April 1990.

It is therefore not surprising that 26 respondents were unable to give this detailed information for three school years. However, 82 respondents did give full responses, representing 68 per cent of the 120 LEAs in England and Wales. In some cases these were estimated figures. The total numbers of instrumental teachers employed in these 82 LEAs are given in Table 2.3.

Table 2.3 **Reported numbers of FTE instrumental teachers in 1989/90, 1990/91 and 1991/92 (82 LEAs)**

Instrumental Area Taught	1989/90	1990/91	1991/92	Change from 1989/90 to 1991/92	
				N	%
strings	996.0	962.0	941.5	-54.5	- 5.5
woodwind	624.0	610.2	601.0	-23.0	- 3.7
brass	514.6	498.0	467.5	-47.1	- 9.2
percussion	70.5	70.3	74.6	+ 4.1	+ 5.8
harp	13.4	13.6	14.0	+ 0.6	+ 4.5
guitar	97.4	90.4	91.5	- 5.9	- 6.1
piano/keyboard	76.5	70.7	76.7	+ 0.2	+ 0.3
recorders	22.8	23.5	25.4	+ 2.6	+11.4
voice	27.4	26.5	27.4	0.0	0.0
steel band	14.5	14.7	15.7	+ 1.2	+ 8.3
Indian instruments*	19.0	18.8	18.8	- 0.2	- 1.1
other teachers	47.5	42.4	40.3	- 7.2	-15.2
Total	2523.6	2441.1	2394.4	-129.2	- 5.1

* The Indian instruments included here are sitar, tabla and harmonium.

The information displayed in Table 2.3 confirms that there has been a small but steady decrease in overall staffing for the three-year period. Some areas of provision have shown greater decreases than others, and a few show a slight increase in teaching staff.

In the previous NFER study, Cleave and Dust estimated that 84 per cent of the FTE instrumental teaching force worked in three main instrumental families: strings (40 per cent) woodwind (24 per cent) and brass (20 per cent). This percentage has remained remarkably consistent from 1985/86 to 1991/92, when the present survey revealed that 84 per cent of the teaching force was employed in the three areas: strings (39 per cent), woodwind (25 per cent) and brass (20 per cent). It is also apparent that strings, brass and woodwind have experienced the largest staff reductions in the past three years. Taken together, cuts in these areas account for 96 per cent of the overall loss in staff from 1989/90 to 1991/92. This is, of course, to be expected because these areas represent by far the largest proportion of instrumental staff. Other areas showing small overall losses between these years were: guitar, other teachers (including teachers of musicianship, theory and advisory teachers offering support for children with special educational needs, multicultural projects and general classroom music support), and a very small loss experienced in teaching staff for the sitar, tabla and harmonium.

Areas showing small staffing gains were: percussion, harp, piano/ keyboard, recorders and steel band. Staffing for vocal tuition was expected to be the same in 1991/92 as in 1989/90.

Staffing changes reported by different types of LEA

The overall totals for FTE instrumental staff shown in Table 2.3 are somewhat misleading since they mask considerable differences between LEAs. Two LEAs had lost all their teaching staff, amounting to 40 FTE in one case and 23 in another. One large metropolitan district had cut 24 teaching posts, representing over a third of its teaching force, another had reduced its staffing from 24 to 5.3 FTE, stretching the former budget for the instrumental service to cover music, drama and dance in a new Performing Arts Development Service. Not surprisingly, respondents in services which had suffered such severe staffing cuts reported widespread effects. As one adviser said: 'I feel very negative. Music until this year was positive, with excellence achieved; this is disappearing fast'. Another exclaimed: 'We're fighting for survival'.

On the other hand, some respondents reported staffing increases over the three-year period. One large English county which had developed its service into a music trust, had recruited 16 new FTE staff. Another London borough, which had formed a music agency, reported a gain of 9.3 FTE staff.

There were also large variations in staffing changes between different types of LEA. Of the 82 respondents who gave full information, 28 were from English counties, 28 from metropolitan districts, 13 from London boroughs, seven from Wales, four from islands and two from inner London authorities. Analysis by type of LEA showed that the metropolitan districts had suffered the largest decrease: a total of 111.6 FTE teachers had been lost, representing a 15 per cent decrease in these authorities' total instrumental staff from 1989/90 to 1991/92. The English counties had reduced their staffing by 23.2 FTE posts overall, representing a decrease of two per cent over three years. The other areas, taken together, showed small staffing gains of four FTE (one per cent) from 1989/90 to 1991/92.

Overall numbers of instrumental staff employed

Some respondents gave an overall total for the number of FTE staff employed, although they were unable to supply a breakdown of the total by instrumental group. On the basis of the information supplied by 88 respondents, we were able to estimate the total number of FTE staff employed in England and Wales. The number of FTE staff per school was calculated for each responding LEA. This figure was then 'grossed up' to include estimates for non-responding LEAs of a similar type, based on their size (i.e. number of schools). In 1991/92 (the year for which most responses were available) we would estimate that around 3,500 instrumental teachers will be employed by music services, agencies and trusts in England and Wales. It should be noted that this estimate includes information from the two authorities which had no instrumental staff because their services were closed in 1990 and 1991.

Somewhat surprisingly, the FTE staffing figure estimated by Cleave and Dust for 1985/86 was exactly the same (i.e. 3,500). This would seem to indicate that there has been an overall expansion in staffing in the period between 1985/86 and 1989/90, followed by a recent decline overall between 1989/90 and 1991/92.

Summary

This chapter has confirmed that LEA instrumental music services are currently facing a period of rapid change in terms of both the sources of funding and the overall level of funding available to support instrumental tuition, music centres, youth choirs and orchestras. Metropolitan districts seemed to be most affected by such funding changes. Funding decreases tended to result in staffing losses.

CHANGES IN SOURCES OF FUNDING

- Comparisons with data collected in 1986 showed that there was a marked increase in plural funding for instrumental music services.

- In terms of instrumental tuition, the LEA was the sole reported funding source in 63 per cent of authorities, and was a funding partner in a further 30 per cent. Parents were the sole funding source in two per cent of LEAs, and made some contribution towards the cost of tuition in a further 24 per cent. Schools were the sole funding source in three per cent of LEAs and contributed towards the cost of tuition from their delegated budgets in a further 14 per cent.

- In terms of the funding for music centres, youth choirs, and orchestras in 104 authorities, the LEA was the sole funding source in 50 per cent and a funding partner in a further 43 per cent. Parents were the sole funding source for these activities in two per cent of authorities and made a contribution in a further 38 per cent of LEAs. Schools were a funding partner in five per cent of LEAs and fundraising contributed in 15 per cent.

- Twenty-seven per cent of respondents reported that the proportions of funding obtained from different sources had changed in the past five years. The main trend was towards a decrease in funding from the LEA and an increase in funding from parents.

CHANGES IN LEVELS OF FUNDING
(from 1989/90 to 1990/91)

- Changes in overall funding for instrumental music services from 1989/90 to 1990/91 were reported in 44 per cent of LEAs.

- Thirty-four per cent of LEAs reported decreases in funding, most of which were either metropolitan districts or London authorities.

- The main causes of funding decreases were cuts in education budgets. Thirteen respondents reported that these cuts resulted from the imposition, or threat, of community charge capping.

- One LEA cut its funding for instrumental music completely from September 1990.

- The two main effects of funding cuts were: reductions in staffing, and reductions in stocks of musical instruments.

- Ten per cent of LEAs reported increases in funding.

- The most frequently reported cause of increased funding was revenue raised from parents and schools.

- Music services had used extra funds to increase staffing, improve management structures, serve more pupils and form new youth orchestras/choirs.

CHANGES IN LEVELS OF FUNDING
(from 1990/91 to 1991/92)

- Changes in funding from 1990/91 to 1991/92 showed a similar pattern to that reported for the previous year.

- Changes in funding were identified in 45 per cent of responding LEAs.

- Thirty-eight per cent of LEAs reported decreases in funding, most of which were either metropolitan districts or London authorities.

- Nineteen per cent of LEAs suffered successive budget cuts in both 1990/91 and 1991/92.

- One LEA cut its funding for instrumental services completely with effect from September 1991, the second to do so in the period covered by the survey.

- Six respondents (6 per cent) predicted increases in funding, three of whom had also reported an increase in the previous year.

CHANGES IN THE NEXT FIVE YEARS

- Nearly half (44 per cent) of the respondents said they knew of further changes in funding for instrumental music which would take effect in the next five years.

- The most frequently mentioned change (affecting 31 per cent of LEAs) was the delegation of centrally held funds for instrumental music to schools under LMS.

- Other predicted changes affecting instrumental provision were: a reduction in LEA budgets due to schools opting out, further increases in parental contributions and the formation of trusts and agencies to run instrumental services.

STAFFING CHANGES
(from 1989/90 to 1991/92)

- Eighty-two LEAs gave full information on staffing levels for a three-year period, although in some cases these were estimated figures.

- Total staffing levels had decreased by 129.2 FTE, a drop of five per cent overall from 1989/90 to 1991/92.

- Three instrumental families (strings, brass and woodwind) accounted for 84 per cent of the total instrumental teaching force. These areas also showed the largest decrease in staffing from 1989/90 to 1991/92.

- Other areas showing small staffing losses were guitar, Indian instruments and 'other teaching staff' (including advisory teachers). Small staffing gains were reported for percussion, harp, piano/keyboard, recorders and steel band.

- There were considerable differences between LEAs in terms of staffing gains and losses. One authority which had cut its service entirely had lost 40 FTE posts. At the other extreme, an LEA music trust had recruited new staff, amounting to an increase of 16 FTE over three years.

- An analysis by type of LEA showed that metropolitan districts had lost the greatest number of staff on average, reporting a decrease in staffing of 15 per cent from 1989/90 to 1991/92.

- It is estimated that around 3,500 FTE instrumental staff will be employed in England and Wales in 1991/92 (excluding private tutors).

- The number of FTE instrumental staff estimated to be employed in 1985/86 was the same as in 1991/92. This finding, together with the reported drop in FTE staffing from 1989/90 indicates that the service has experienced an expansion followed by contraction in the years between the two NFER surveys.

3 Instrumental Tuition and Musical Instruments

Introduction

This chapter is primarily concerned with the provision of instrumental tuition (including voice) and of the musical instruments themselves.

The chapter begins by considering the role of instrumental music, and whether there has been a change in its perceived role between 1986, the time of the previous NFER survey, and 1991.

The next section of the chapter provides evidence on the range of musical instruments taught and when tuition begins (i.e. in the primary or secondary phase of education). The number of music centres, and the types of activities they offer, is discussed. This is followed by information on the number of schools and children receiving regular instrumental tuition. The criteria used by music services to select schools and pupils are examined.

The final part of the chapter considers the availability of musical instruments, sheet music, equipment and sundries; and finds out who is generally responsible for providing these items for children receiving instrumental tuition. The chapter ends with a summary of the main points.

The role of instrumental music

The questionnaire asked respondents: 'What do you see as the main role of the existing instrumental service/agency in your LEA?'. The majority (102, 94 per cent) of respondents answered this question, many enclosing documents which gave a statement of the aims of their service, agency or trust.

In most cases, respondents listed a variety of aims. An attempt was made to categorise these answers according to their main emphasis. This yielded five categories ranging from a concern with providing a service to schools, to the development of individual musical potential and talent. The different types of response are given below, presented in order of frequency.

a) **Providing a music tuition service to schools.**

This was a very simple and straightforward aim expressed by just over half the respondents to the survey. Many stressed the importance of offering a high quality service: for example, 'to provide a coherent, well planned and organised instrumental music service to schools'. The other important element was a concern to provide instrumental tuition to as many schools and pupils as resources would allow. Some respondents emphasised their ability to offer a variety of musical experiences such as individual and group tuition, workshops and lessons, and tuition in a wide range of instruments. For a minority, the emphasis was on stimulating new demand for tuition from parents and children as well as from schools.

b) **Enhancing classroom music.**

A fifth of respondents expressed the role of instrumental music tuition in terms of support for classroom music: for example, 'to support schools and help them to deliver a broad and balanced music curriculum'. Some respondents mentioned specific types of support such as class music workshops for primary schools or tuition to GCSE and 'A' level syllabuses. Others drew attention to the potential role of instrumental music in helping teachers to provide music education as part of the National Curriculum.

c) **Providing children with experience of music-making.**
A small group of respondents saw the main purpose of their service as providing children with opportunities for making music. The emphasis here was on the practical experience of music-making. Respondents drew attention to the pleasure experienced by children making music, either individually or in groups/ensembles: for example 'To introduce students of all ages to the joy and fulfilment of making "real" music'.

d) **Teaching specific skills.**
A minority of respondents said that the main purpose of their service, trust or agency was to teach the specific skills associated with playing a musical instrument. For example: 'to teach music systematically through the means of a specific instrument in order to develop specific skills'.

e) **Developing pupil potential.**
A small number of respondents believed that instrumental tuition should be primarily concerned with developing the potential of children with a particular facility for music. For example: 'to offer extended opportunities to musically gifted pupils'.

A comparison with data gathered by Cleave and Dust in the previous NFER survey shows a substantial change in emphasis between 1986 and 1991. Cleave and Dust also identified five broad definitions of the purpose of the instrumental music service: teaching specific skills (more than a third of respondents); developing pupil potential (nearly a quarter); providing experience of music-making; enhancing music education generally; and contributing to the all-round development of the individual. (The last three categories each represented the views of a small minority of respondents).

When comparing the two analyses, three categories of response are the same in both cases. A fourth category, 'the enhancement of music education generally' is a similar category to that of 'enhancing classroom music-making' in the 1991 analysis, although from the description of this category given by Cleave and Dust, it is apparent that the respondents to the 1991 survey made more specific reference to the type of classroom support they offered, rather than talking about instrumental music enhancing the music curriculum in general terms.

The most marked difference between the analyses of responses obtained in 1986 and 1991 concerns the appearance, in 1991, of a new category representing over half the responses: 'Providing a music tuition service to schools'. Cleave and Dust state that a majority of the respondents to their survey expressed the view that the service should reach as many children as possible, but they were able to subdivide these responses into five categories representing the main purpose of the music service. When analysing the responses to the 1991 survey, it was impossible to put many of the responses into any other category: some respondents simply stated the provision of an instrumental service to schools as their sole aim. It therefore seems likely that there has been a real change in emphasis between 1986 and 1991. A possible explanation for such a change in stated purpose is that the providers of instrumental services are responding to changes introduced in the 1988 Education Reform Act, notably the Local Management of Schools. Schools, rather than individual pupils or the LEA, are now perceived as the main clients of the service and respondents are keen to stress the advantages of quality control and classroom support provided by a centralised service, particularly when their service is under the real or potential threat of competition from private tutors.

Instruments taught

The questionnaire asked respondents to indicate which instruments were taught by their staff in primary and/or secondary schools. The questionnaire gave a list of 28 instruments (including voice) and a category termed 'other instruments'. The total responses from 104 LEAs are given in Table 3.1, which shows the percentage of LEAs offering each type of tuition and compares the 1991 survey results with those obtained in 1986.

The table represents responses from 104 LEAs to the 1991 survey. Three inner London authorities did not respond to this question. One metropolitan district had had its entire service disbanded in 1990, and therefore reported no provision at all. This LEA was not included in the analysis. (In 1986, one LEA was known to have lost its instrumental service, but it did not respond to the survey, and therefore was not represented in any of the quantitative analyses reported in *A Sound Start*).

The 1991 survey results show that the main families of orchestral instruments (brass, woodwind and strings) are well represented among LEAs. Of the brass instruments, trombone was taught in all 104 LEAs, and the trumpet was taught in all LEAs except one metropolitan district. The horn and tuba were taught in the majority of LEAs. The flute and clarinet were the most widely taught woodwind instruments, and most LEAs provided tuition on the oboe. Of the strings, violin and cello were taught everywhere except in one very small authority. A majority of LEAs also offered tuition for viola and double bass.

Over three-quarters of LEAs provided tuition on saxophone, brass band instruments and percussion; and over half of LEAs provided tuition on classical guitar. Although the recorder is widely taught in schools, some respondents pointed out that this was usually taught by classroom teachers rather than specialist instrumental

Table 3.1: Types of instrumental tuition offered by LEAs in 1986/87 and 1990/91

Instruments	% LEAs in 1990/91	% LEAs in 1986/87	% Difference from 1986 to 1991
trombone	100	100	
trumpet	99	100	- 1
flute	99	100	- 1
violin	99	99	
cello	99	99	
clarinet	98	100	- 2
saxophone	97	99	- 2
horn	96	100	- 4
oboe	95	100	- 5
viola	95	99	- 4
tuba	92	99	- 7
double bass	92	98	- 6
bassoon	91	100	- 9
brass band instruments	88	90	- 2
percussion	80	86	- 6
guitar (classical)	66	68	- 2
recorders	48	48	
guitar (electric/bass)	45	33	+12
piano	37	38	- 1
voice	34	27	+ 7
keyboard synthesiser/electric	33	30	+ 3
steel band	27	18	+ 9
harp	21	24	- 3
tabla	18	8	+10
harmonium	17	8	+ 9
sitar	15	8	+ 7
early instruments, other than recorder	11	19	- 8
other instruments	5	9	- 4
	(N = 104)	(N = 93)	

teachers. Despite this, nearly half of LEAs offered some instrumental teaching for recorders, often for more advanced work or for ensembles. Other early instruments, such as the viol, carnamusen, sackbut, lute and rackett, were taught in a small minority of LEAs.

The table shows that over a third of LEAs provided piano tuition. This was more common in London authorities than in Welsh or English counties or the metropolitan districts. Tuition on synthesiser/ keyboards was almost at the same level as piano tuition. This is probably due to the fact that keyboards have become popular classroom instruments, they are less expensive than pianos and children learning on keyboards can more easily be taught in groups.

Another modern instrument, the electric or bass guitar, was taught in 45 per cent of LEAs, and was most commonly taught in London and the metropolitan districts.

Just over a third of authorities offered vocal or choral tuition. Again, a high proportion of London authorities offered this kind of provision. Less than one in five English or Welsh authorities offered tuition for voice.

Tuition on the harp was provided by just over a fifth of LEAs. As might be expected, this instrument was most commonly taught in Wales, with seven of the eight Welsh authorities providing tuition on the harp. Harp tuition was offered in less than a fifth of English counties and metropolitan districts. No island or inner London authority provided tuition on the harp.

A minority of LEAs provided tuition on instruments for the performance of music outside the Western tradition (steel band, tabla, harmonium and sitar). Steel band tuition was provided by about a quarter of LEAs. It was most commonly taught in London authorities: no Welsh or island authority offered tuition for steel pans. Provision of tuition on Indian instruments followed a similar pattern, being most commonly taught in London authorities, much less common in English counties or metropolitan districts and not offered in any of the island or Welsh authorities.

Tuition on other instruments was reported in a small minority of cases. These included folk guitar in one London borough and 'Russian' instruments such as balalaika, dorma and guissli in a metropolitan district. This latter authority also reported tuition in African drum and song styles. In some LEAs, general music tuition was offered, for example: theory, composition, general musicianship and kindermusik (a course of various activities for young children aiming to develop musical literacy, aural and coordination skills). A few authorities also offered music therapy.

Ranges of instruments taught in different types of LEA

As explained above, the questionnaire offered respondents the opportunity to report on their provision of tuition for a wide range of instruments, including voice and 'other' instruments, amounting to a maximum of 29 different categories of musical provision.

An analysis of the range of instruments taught by different types of LEA yielded some interesting variations. When analysed by type of LEA, the average number of instruments taught ranged from 16 in the small island authorities and in Wales, to 21 in London. Counties taught an average of 17 instruments and the average for metropolitan districts was 18. Some of these differences in the ranges of instruments taught seem to be associated with the size of LEA (the small islands offer the smallest range of instruments), and with provision of 'non-Western' instrumental tuition (which was most common in London authorities).

There were also considerable differences between individual LEAs, with the smallest number of instruments in any single LEA (nine) being taught in a small metropolitan district, and the largest (28) in its large metropolitan neighbour.

Changes from 1986 to 1991

Table 3.1 records the findings of the two NFER surveys and the differences in the proportions of LEAs offering tuition on each instrument.

It is difficult to state whether small differences between the figures reflect real changes over time, or are due to slight differences in the two samples of LEAs. However, as in both cases, the question gained high response rates (86 per cent in 1986, 87 per cent in 1991) large percentage changes in provision are most probably the result of trends over time.

As might be expected, the largest decreases in provision between 1986/87 and 1990/91 are found in the three main orchestral groups (particularly tuba, bassoon, double bass and oboe). There has also been a drop in the percentage of LEAs offering tuition for percussion and early instruments (excluding recorder).

The main increases in provision are apparent in modern instruments and those for the performance of music outside the Western tradition. Electric/bass guitar tuition shows the greatest increase of all, being offered in just under half of LEAs responding to the 1991 survey. In the previous study, Cleave and Dust (1989) identified a trend away from piano tuition in favour of tuition on synthesisers and keyboards reporting that some authorities: 'planned to increase pupils' opportunities to work on electric keyboards'. This trend appears to have continued, although keyboards have not yet overtaken piano tuition in popularity.

'Non-Western' instrumental provision appears to have increased, although care must be taken in interpretation here, because the 1991 analysis includes nine inner London LEAs, which were not in existence at the time of the 1986 survey. When these authorities are excluded, there is still a small increase in provision for steel band and tabla, and for sitar and harmonium: in the case of these latter two instruments, there has been a rise of over seven per cent in the authorities offering such tuition.

Trends in staffing and provision

In Chapter 2, information was provided on changes in staffing levels for different types of instrument. This showed an overall drop in FTE staff over a three year period (1989/90 to 1991/92), with the greatest losses experienced for strings, woodwind and brass, and smaller losses for Indian instruments and other teachers. Small FTE gains were reported for percussion, harp, piano/keyboard, recorder and steel band.

The information given in Table 3.1 shows changes in the percentage of authorities offering at least some tuition on particular instruments between 1986/87 and 1990/91. The two sets of data reported in Chapters 2 and 3 are not directly comparable because they are based on different types of information, although both provide insights into trends in provision over time. Taken together, they indicate that tuition on instruments in the the three main orchestral 'families' (strings, woodwinds and brass) is provided by most authorities, although many have reduced the number of staff and/or the hours worked by staff teaching these instruments. Overall, authorities appear to have been able to sustain some provision for these instruments whilst reducing staffing levels, because these three instrumental families account for the large majority of staff employed. However, smaller LEAs have less flexibility in this regard, since even small reductions in their staffing may lead to a loss of teachers with specialist expertise.

In terms of particular instruments, there has been a recent reduction in the number of FTE guitar teachers, but there are now more authorities offering tuition on the **electric/bass** guitar than in 1986/87. A similar pattern is evident for the sitar, tabla and harmonium. This would seem to indicate a rise in staffing after 1986, followed by a more recent reduction. On the other hand, there have been recent small FTE staffing gains for harp and percussion but the proportion of authorities offering such tuition has decreased slightly since 1986.

Instruments taught in the primary and secondary stage of education

As well as asking which instruments were taught by members of instrumental services, agencies and trusts, the questionnaire asked respondents to indicate at what stage such tuition usually began i.e. primary (years 1 to 6) or secondary (years 7-13). One hundred and four LEAs responded to this question and their answers are represented in Figure 3.1.

Figure 3.1 shows the number of LEAs providing tuition on each instrument in 1991, and the number beginning in the primary and secondary stage. No instrument is taught exclusively at the secondary stage, and for most instruments tuition starts predominantly at the primary stage. The only instrument for which tuition begins exclusively at the primary stage is the violin. This accords with both the popularity of the instrument and the belief that tuition on the violin must begin early. The methods developed by Shinichi Suzuki and Sheila Nelson (amongst others) for teaching violin to very young children have become popular in this country and several respondents reported the use of these approaches in their LEAs. Scaled-down versions of the violin have been designed for use by young children.

Figure 3.1   Instrumental tuition offered and the stage at which children begin (104 LEAs)

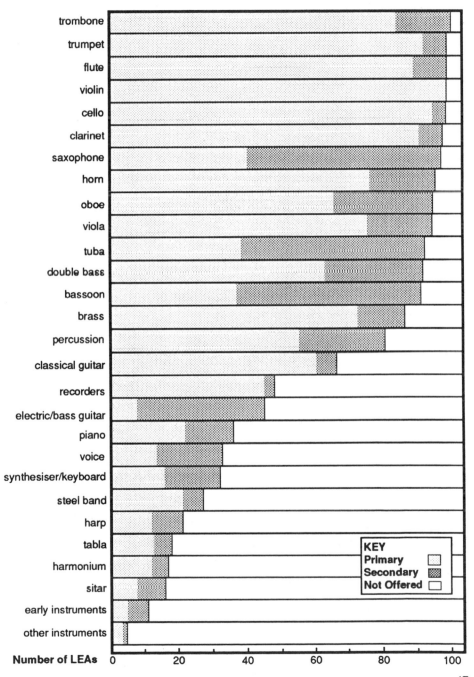

Instruments which most providing LEAs began teaching in the secondary sector were: saxophone, tuba, bassoon, electric or bass guitar, voice and early instruments. The later start for these instruments is probably due to a combination of factors. Younger children are unable to cope with the physical demands of large instruments and these particular instruments are not generally available in reduced sizes. Some of the listed instruments are expensive and only a small stock may be available for use by beginners. In addition, some instruments (such as the electric guitar and saxophone) may be particularly popular with older students.

In the previous NFER survey, Cleave and Dust reported similar findings with regard to the instruments listed above. However, their findings showed that keyboards were generally taught to older children. It would seem that not only has the proportion of LEAs providing tuition for keyboards increased since 1986, but it has also become more common practice to begin tuition on keyboards in the primary school.

Music centres

The role and operation of music centres was discussed in detail in *A Sound Start*. The purpose of this section is to consider what, if any, changes have taken place five years after that research was carried out.

Music centres (or music schools) are a feature of instrumental service organisation in a majority of LEAs. In some cases these are administrative centres rather than centres of musical activity, although they can fulfil both these functions. Most of the larger

LEAs have a number of regional or area centres. Very few music centres are built for the sole purpose of music education and many music centre activities take place in schools - after school hours, at weekends and during the school holidays.

In inner London, all the authorities share the facilities of one large music centre, which was established to maintain music activities following the demise of the ILEA. This centre, known as the Centre for Young Musicians (CYM) offers a wide range of activities for the pupils who attend from 13 LEAs. Four of the inner London authorities also reported that they had their own music centres. (Further information on the operation of the CYM is given in Chapter 6.)

Eighty-eight respondents gave information on the number of pupils from their areas attending music centres in 1989/90 and 1990/91. In some cases, respondents were unable to give precise figures so they provided estimates instead.

On the basis of this information, it was possible to estimate the total number of pupils (including those from infant, primary and secondary schools, sixth form centres and special schools) attending music centres in England and Wales. The estimated overall number of pupils attending music centres was around 147,500 in 1990/91, representing about two per cent of the total school population.

Table 3.2 gives the incidence of music centres in 91 LEAs in England and Wales. The responses from inner London authorities have been excluded from the analysis in order to allow a more direct comparison to be made between the results of the two NFER surveys.

Table 3.2: Incidence of music centres in 91 LEAs in England and Wales
1990/91 (information from the 1986 survey is given in brackets)

LEAs	No. of LEAs	Total No. of Centres	Average No. of Centres per LEA	Range
English counties	35 (34)	278 (232)	7.9 (6.8)	1-19 (1-30)
Metropolitan districts	28 (29)	132 (96)	4.7 (3.3)	1-19 (1-10)
London boroughs	18 (17)	32 (43)	1.8 (2.6)	1- 7 (1-9)
Island authorities	3 (3)	6 (4)	2.0 (1.3)	1- 4 (1-2)
Wales	7 (7)	35 (33)	5.0 (4.7)	1-14 (1-12)
Overall average			5.3 (4.5)	
Totals	91 (90)	483 (408)		1-19 (1-30)

The table includes LEAs which had one or more music centres. In addition to those included in the table, three other respondents replied to this question by saying that there were no music centres in their authorities. (These have not been included in the table to enable comparisons to be made between the two NFER studies.) In one case, the lack of music centres was due to the closure of the entire music service in 1990.

The table shows that there was a total of 483 music centres operating in 91 LEAs in 1990/91. English counties tended to have a higher than average number of music centres, with the London boroughs and island authorities having the fewest per LEA.

From the information gathered in their survey of 1986, Cleave and Dust reported that 90 LEAs had a total of 408 music centres, giving an average of 4.5 centres per authority. The apparent slight increase in music centres between the two surveys is most evident in metropolitan districts, which had three centres on average in 1986 and nearly five in 1991. Although small apparent changes may be due to differences in the two samples, it is probable that there has been a slight expansion in the number of music centres between 1986 and 1991.

Music centre activities

Respondents to the 1991 questionnaire survey were asked to indicate which of a number of different types of activity were available to children at music centres in their authorities. Eight different types of activity were listed in the question, together with an additional category of 'other activities'. The question used the same list of common music centre activities in 1991 as in the 1986 questionnaire. The results obtained in the two surveys are shown in Table 3.3.

The table shows results from 90 LEAs in 1986/87 and 92 in 1990/91. The inner London authorities have been excluded from the 1991 analysis for two reasons: first, responses were difficult to interpret in cases where authorities had both their own music centre and pupils from the authority attending the CYM; second, the exclusion of these authorities allows for a fairer comparison between the two surveys conducted in 1986 and 1991. (However, it was interesting to note that several respondents from inner London reported that the CYM provided all eight listed types of activity.)

The table shows that, in 1991, all LEAs offered opportunities for youth ensembles, bands and choirs to meet and rehearse at music centres. Over two-thirds offered opportunities for group tuition, choirs, theory and aural work. Over half provided individual tuition and general musicianship. Help with composition and improvisation was provided by over a third of authorities at their music centres. About one in five LEAs also offered other activities.

Table 3.3: **Music centre activities provided by English and Welsh LEAs in 1986/87 and 1990/91**

Activity	LEAs providing the activity		% difference
	% in 1986/87	% in 1990/91	
Ensembles, bands and orchestras	100	100	
Group tuition	73	73	
Choirs	52	68	+16
Theory	59	66	+ 7
Aural	51	66	+15
Individual tuition	66	65	- 1
Musicianship	50	59	+ 9
Composition/ improvisation	29	34	+ 5
Other activities	19	22	+ 3
Total no. of LEAs	90	92	

The most commonly mentioned additional activities were: music technology (including opportunities for using computers, electronic instruments and recording studios) and early years' provision (such as kindermusik and 'music reading classes for infant violinists'). Some authorities used their centres to provide opportunities for other performing arts' work, such as dance, drama and music theatre. A few respondents mentioned that their centres provided tuition for students studying 'A' level courses. In some schools, very few candidates register to study 'A' level music. The provision of 'A' level tuition at a music centre therefore supplements the provision available in schools. Other activities provided by one or two authorities included: early music; class singing; hand bells; Russian and Indian dance; staff in-service provision and practice facilities for an OAP orchestra.

The 'menu' of activities offered varied considerably, with 17 respondents reporting that their music centres offered all the listed activities, and 15 respondents reporting that their music centres offered only one or two.

A comparison between the results obtained in the two surveys shows an apparent increase in the proportion of LEAs offering certain activities. As would be expected, the largest increases are evident for some of the activities which were most frequently reported in 1986/87, i.e. choirs (a change of 16 per cent), and aural tuition (15 per cent). It is possible that the increase in choirs may be linked to the legislation regarding charging for school activities, which allows a charge to be levied for instrumental tuition, but not for vocal tuition taking place within school time (see also Chapter 5). The increases in the number of music centres offering aural activities is perhaps best explained by the introduction of the GCSE music examination in 1986, which placed a strong emphasis on aural work, as do other music examinations.

Although it is problematic to draw direct comparisons between results obtained in the two surveys (for the reasons given above) it does seem likely that more LEA music centres were offering a wider range of activities in 1991 when compared with 1986.

Level of provision in schools

Respondents were asked to state what proportion of schools and pupils (primary, secondary and special) in their authorities were receiving regular tuition (i.e. once a week or more) on one or more instruments, from an LEA service, trust or agency. The definition of 'primary' included infant, first and middle deemed primary schools. The definition of 'secondary' included middle deemed secondary, upper schools and sixth form colleges.

Number of pupils receiving tuition

Sixty-nine respondents were able to give figures for the percentage of pupils in their authorities receiving regular instrumental tuition in 1989/90 and 1990/91. (In many cases these were estimates.) Using information about the school populations in each LEA, drawn from statistics compiled by the Department of Education and Science, it was possible to calculate the approximate numbers of children receiving instrumental tuition in all responding LEAs. These figures were then used as a basis to estimate the number of pupils receiving tuition in those authorities which did not provide the information, so that estimates for the numbers of pupils receiving instrumental tuition in England and Wales could be reported.

There are approximately 7,300,000 children attending maintained schools in England and Wales. On the basis of information received from 69 authorities (58 per cent of all the LEAs in England and Wales) it is estimated that the total number of pupils receiving instrumental tuition was approximately 467,500 in 1990/91 (between six and seven per cent of the total school population.) This estimate represents a slight fall from the number receiving tuition in the previous school year, which we would estimate to be 486,000.

As might be expected, the percentages given for pupils receiving tuition varied considerably between LEAs. Participation rates tended to be highest in the London area (around 11 per cent) and lowest in the English counties (between five and six per cent). This variation is probably associated with the geographical area of the LEAs concerned. Services based in large counties tend to find it more difficult to reach a high proportion of pupils because they are distributed across a wider geographical area.

On average, provision was split fairly evenly between primary and secondary pupils: pupils in special schools were less commonly served, with only about one per cent of the total population of special school pupils receiving instrumental tuition in 1990/91.

Number of schools receiving tuition

Estimates of the number of pupils receiving tuition provide a measure of the extent of music services, but the question arises as to whether services are spread equally among schools or are concentrated on larger numbers of children in a few schools. Ninety-five respondents gave information on the percentage of schools receiving regular visits from peripatetic instrumental staff. On the basis of these responses, we would estimate that approximately 17,000 schools were receiving such visits in 1990/91, representing about 64 per cent of the total number of maintained schools in England and Wales. The percentage of schools receiving tuition tended to be highest in the island authorities (around 90 per cent) and in Wales (around 85 per cent); services, trusts and agencies based in the English counties tended to reach fewest of their schools (around 60 per cent).

On average, music services provided tuition to a higher proportion of secondary than primary schools, and to few special schools. The relative estimated figures for England and Wales in 1990/91 were: primary, 63 per cent; secondary, 97 per cent; and special, 16 per cent. A comparison with figures for the previous year revealed a slight increase of about one per cent in provision to primary and special schools and a slight decrease in provision to the secondary sector from 1989/90 to 1990/91.

Comparisons with results obtained in previous surveys

It is difficult to obtain precise figures on the proportions of schools and pupils receiving instrumental tuition from an LEA service in previous years. This is probably due to the fact that some LEAs simply do not collate this information. However, a number of estimates do exist. The Gulbenkian report on the training of musicians published in 1978 suggested that 'about five per cent' of pupils were receiving instrumental tuition. In 1984, an unpublished HMI inquiry estimated that between four and eight per cent of pupils received tuition. Cleave and Dust, on the basis of their survey conducted in 1986, estimated that of 362,000 children were learning to play an instrument (between five and six per cent of the total school population at the time). In terms of schools, they state: 'the figures revealed that the average LEA was providing instrumental tuition in about 65 per cent of its schools'. They also report that most LEAs provided tuition to 90 per cent or more of their secondary schools and to some (i.e. less than 90 per cent) of their primaries. An HMI document (GB, DES 1991a), reporting on inspections carried out between 1982 and 1989, stated that approximately one third of primary schools were receiving 'some kind of support from peripatetic instrumental teachers'.

Taken together, these surveys and reports estimate that around five to six per cent of pupils were receiving instrumental tuition between 1978 and 1986. In comparison, the results from the 1991 survey showed an apparent increase to between six and seven per cent. Does this, then, represent a real rise in provision in the past five years?

Considerable caution must be exercised in drawing any such conclusion. The results reported in the two NFER surveys are 'grossed up' figures, based to a large extent on estimations. The margin for error may be wider than the apparent difference in results; therefore, it is difficult to conclude that there has been a large expansion in the number of pupils receiving tuition between 1985/86 and 1990/91. It does, however, seem likely that there has been general increase in the percentage of primary schools receiving tuition in England and Wales.

On the other hand, the fact that the same estimated total number of FTE instrumental staff was reported in the two NFER studies would lead to an expectation that the 1991 figures should show about the same number of pupils and schools receiving tuition. The apparent increase in the number of pupils and schools served (especially between the two NFER surveys) could be due to a number of factors.

First, it is possible that the 1986 survey gave a slightly low estimate of the number of pupils receiving tuition, because the results did not include the ILEA (a very large authority which was not able to provide this information at the time). It is apparent from the 1991 survey results that provision in inner London tends to be higher than average. If the 1986 survey had included the large population within ILEA, this might have resulted in a slightly higher overall estimate for provision in 1986.

A second possibility is that LEA services, trusts and agencies have increased the participation rate by increasing the number of pupils within tuition groups, increasing efficiency, and/or by reducing the time given to each pupil.

The survey collected information on changes in the size of tuition groups. The questionnaire asked respondents if the average size of groups taught by instrumental staff had changed in the last five years. Thirty-seven respondents (34 per cent) reported an increase in the number of pupils per group. These increases were due to a combination of factors, such as: the need to redistribute the service to more schools because of the influence of LMS (see also Chapter 5); an increase in the demand for tuition; the need to improve efficiency; a move from individual to group tuition; and an attempt to maintain the level of provision despite staffing cuts. A few respondents also mentioned that their staff had received support and training to help them cope with teaching larger groups.

Six respondents reported decreases in the size of tuition groups due to two main factors: the need to change from group to individual tuition in order to charge for tuition (see also Chapter 5); and a wish to increase the quality of tuition offered to each pupil, especially those studying for GCSE and 'A' level.

Without comparative information on the efficiency of instrumental teachers, it is impossible to comment on any recent improvement on this area. However, service managers would probably argue that they have improved the efficiency of their services (see Chapter 4 for information on quality control and the number of pupils taught by each teacher).

The survey did not ask about the length of lessons, although there were some anecdotal reports of a trend towards a shortening of lessons in order to enable peripatetic staff to reach more pupils and schools.

The estimates given here are for the tuition provided by instrumental services, agencies and trusts. They do not include the tuition provided by private tutors, the level of which is, at present, unknown. It is hoped that research currently being undertaken by Louise Gibbs at Goldsmith's College, University of London, will shed some light on the number of such teachers and the level of tuition they provide.

Selection of schools

The questionnaire asked respondents to describe how schools were selected to receive instrumental tuition from an LEA service, trust or agency. Most respondents explained that a variety of factors were taken into account and some said that policies varied according to the sector (for example, primary, secondary, special) the type of instrument, or the area of the LEA.

Over a third of respondents said that schools were not selected: the system operating in their LEAs could be described as 'fair shares' (i.e. an allocation of time or money related to the number of pupils in a school) and/or 'demand led' (i.e. schools and parents obtained tuition on request). The main influences here were Local Management of Schools (which had prompted heads in many areas to request an equitable sharing of LEA services amongst schools), and the existence of agencies and trusts, charging schools or parents for tuition. Some LEAs had a system whereby all schools received some tuition (or funding representing their 'share' of the former instrumental budget) but schools could buy in extra tuition from the service or agency (see Chapter 5). Many other respondents said that, although selection existed at present, their LEAs were moving to a 'formula funding' allocation for all schools in the near future.

The main factor taken into account in the LEAs with some form of selection were historical patterns of allocation, and, to a lesser effect, the perceived level of support for music in the school.

Historical patterns of provision, often dating back to local government reorganisation in 1974, were reported to be affecting the distribution of instrumental music tuition to schools in different areas within about a third of LEAs. Some of the respondents from inner London authorities pointed out that provision in their LEAs was a result of decisions taken by the ILEA: 'At present we are sustaining exactly the same pattern of instrumental tuition as occurred under ILEA. It is unclear how ILEA decided where provision should be distributed'. A majority of the respondents who said that historical patterns were affecting current provision explained that change to a more equitable system was under way, for example: 'Provision up to now has been *ad hoc* and by demand. We are currently instituting policies designed to even out provision but this will take time'. A few expressed their frustration with the existing pattern of provision but said that a lack of resources was limiting their ability to bring about change.

Sixteen respondents mentioned that the level of support for music in the school was taken into account when deciding which schools should receive tuition. This was usually assessed on the basis of the head's attitude to music. One adviser said schools were selected on the basis of 'requests from a concerned headteacher or head of music'. Another explained that selection was influenced by 'enthusiasm and back-up to the service from within the school'.

Another policy, adopted by a small number of LEAs, was to target the service on particular 'clusters' or 'pyramids' of primary and secondary schools. The intention here was to ensure continuity of tuition between primary and secondary schools, and to organise provision in a practical way (so that one teacher could visit several neighbouring schools in succession). One respondent explained that the clustering system adopted in his authority worked by allocating one teacher (either strings or woodwind) to each of a group of primary schools. The secondary school was allocated a number of teachers offering a 'full range' of instrumental tuition. In another authority, the clustering system was targeted on groups of small schools. The respondent explained that historically such schools had not received any instrumental tuition. The clustering system was introduced in order to spread provision to these schools in a cost-effective way.

Selection of pupils

Once a school has been selected, or has selected itself for instrumental provision, the question arises as to which children should actually receive tuition. In almost all cases (except where parents paid directly for tuition) some form of pupil selection took place. Indeed, competition for tuition places may have become stronger recently as some services are spread more thinly over a larger number of schools.

Who selects?

In most of the LEAs surveyed, the selection of pupils was a joint decision between instrumental and school staff. In the primary school, the person consulted was usually the class teacher and/or the head. In secondary schools, discussions usually took place with the head of the music or performing arts department. In some cases the decision was equally weighted between school and instrumental service; in others one or other party made the final decision. For example, it was fairly common practice for schools to propose a number of pupils for consideration by instrumental staff. The peripatetic teacher was then responsible for making a final selection, often based on an audition or aural test. On the other hand, in some LEAs the school was responsible for the choice, after taking advice from peripatetic teachers (for example, about a child's suitability for a particular instrument).

A small minority of respondents reported that parents were very much part of the selection process. For example: 'Parents are involved in discussion with teacher and head. Pupils are selected after this process'. However, it was usual practice for parents to be consulted after an initial selection had been made. One respondent reported that his agency had successfully trialled a new approach whereby an extended selection process was carried out over half a term, involving teachers, parents and pupils.

A minority of respondents said that pupils were given tuition solely or mainly on request. In many cases, these were LEAs which charged parents for tuition. Some pointed out that no LEA-wide policy was in force: schools made their own selections of children to receive instrumental tuition.

Selection criteria

Most respondents said that some form of selection policy was in operation in their LEAs. Most also reported that more than one factor was taken into account when choosing which children should receive lessons. The most commonly mentioned criteria were: musical ability, interest and enthusiasm for learning an instrument, physical suitability, and parental support.

Musical ability

Musical ability was reported to be a factor in pupil selection in most LEAs. There were two main approaches used: a test of musical ability or a more general assessment of musicality usually based on a child's response in classroom music lessons.

About two fifths of respondents said that children were tested for musical ability or potential, often using commercially available aural tests, such as the 'Bentley' or 'Janet Mills' test. Some used tests designed by the instrumental staff themselves: for example, a test of 'ability to differentiate higher and lower of two notes, and to clap a simple rhythm'. A few LEAs preferred to ask children to 'audition' for a member of the peripatetic staff.

General musical ability or potential was usually assessed by the classroom teacher, who then recommended children to instrumental staff. For example, one respondent explained that 'musical promise' was taken into account in his authority, demonstrated by interest and ability in class music and aptitude in playing the recorder.

Interest and enthusiasm

Interest and enthusiasm for learning an instrument were important attributes as far as a third of respondents were concerned. Some stressed that, although other factors were taken into account, evidence of 'commitment enthusiasm and perseverance' would weigh heavily in a child's favour. Learning an instrument requires a fair amount of dedication from children and a commitment to practice between lessons. Music teachers are acutely aware of the need for perseverance (a characteristic which two respondents described as 'stickability') and look for this in children selected to receive tuition.

Physical suitability

About a fifth of respondents said that physical suitability was a factor in selection for particular instruments. One respondent sent guidelines on selection, which mentioned that ill health (for example, asthma or heart murmur) should not count against pupils, but another said that, in his authority, physical characteristics such as 'size of hands and dental formation' would be taken into account.

Parental support

A small number of respondents said that parental support was considered alongside other factors. As mentioned above, learning an instrument requires perseverance and practice, both of which can be enhanced by supportive parents. In some cases, it was financial support that was required, normally to purchase or hire an instrument.

Availability of instruments

A few respondents also pointed out that the availability of resources (i.e. teachers and/or instruments) was effectively limiting the number of children who could learn an instrument. For example: 'selection is affected by the availability of an instrument. Sharing is not permitted for hygiene and practice reasons'. In such circumstances children were often put onto a waiting list or offered an alternative instrument for tuition.

Musical instruments and equipment

Allocation of instruments

The majority of respondents (92 per cent) reported that their LEA service, trust or agency held a stock of musical instruments for use by pupils. Of these, most allocated the instruments either to pupils (40 per cent) or to schools (25 per cent). The rest gave stocks to a combination of pupils, schools and/or music centres. A minority said they differentiated according to the type of instruments concerned, reserving better quality instruments for ensembles and bands, or keeping large, expensive items (for example, percussion) at particular centres.

Although a majority of LEA services, trusts or agencies had their own instruments, these were usually limited in terms of both the size of stock and the quality of instruments available. It was therefore not possible for all children receiving tuition to use an LEA- or agency- provided instrument for an extended period.

Fifty-four per cent of the LEAs which had stocks of instruments provided them free of charge to children for an unlimited period of time. Twenty-nine per cent provided instruments without charge for a limited period only, and 13 per cent hired the instruments to pupils. The questionnaire asked whether there was a particular stage at which parents were encouraged to buy an instrument for their child: over two-thirds of respondents said there was. In most cases this took place after a certain period of time, usually when a child had been learning for one or two years. In other authorities, the child's progress and/or their parents' ability to pay were taken into account. A few LEAs simply encouraged parents to purchase instruments 'as soon as possible', whereas others explained that different policies operated according to the expense of the instrument concerned.

In their survey of 1986, Cleave and Dust found that 38 per cent of LEAs provided instruments free of charge for an unlimited period of time. This proportion has risen to 54 per cent in the 1991 survey. This apparent change may be due to the legislation regarding charging for school activities (see also Chapter 6), which has curtailed LEAs' ability to charge for musical instruments.

Responsibility for maintenance and repair of instruments

Maintenance and repair of instruments can be costly, especially where major repairs to expensive instruments are needed. Respondents were asked where the main responsibility for maintenance and repair of LEA- or agency-owned instruments lay. In just over half of cases, the LEA or agency was solely responsible. In the other half, the expense was generally borne by schools or was shared between the LEA or agency and schools. Parents also contributed to these costs in just under a third of LEAs.

Purchase of musical equipment, sheet music and sundries

Respondents were asked to indicate the main providers of equipment (for example, music stands), sheet music, and sundries (for example, strings, reeds, shoulder pads), for pupils receiving instrumental tuition in their authorities. The results from this question are displayed in Table 3.4.

The table shows that the responsibility for providing musical equipment, sheet music and sundries was generally shared between three partners: LEA/agency, schools and parents. In terms of music equipment, the LEA/agency was the main providing body. It was the only source of provision in nearly a third of LEAs and a funding partner in another half. Sheet music tended to be a shared responsibility, with the LEA/agency as a funding partner in a majority of LEAs.

**Table 3.4   Provision of musical equipment, sheet music and sundries.
(103 LEAs)**

Provider	Equipment	Sheet Music	Sundries
	%	%	%
LEA/agency* only	31	19	12
LEA/agency and schools	28	20	5
LEA/agency and parents	9	21	15
LEA/agency, schools and parents	17	23	26
Schools only	13	9	9
Parents only	2	4	22
Schools and parents	-	4	11
Total per cent	100	100	100

*LEA/agency includes music trusts

The provision of sundries was again shared between schools, parents and the LEA/agency; but parents were the main source, contributing towards provision of these items in over three-quarters of LEAs.

It may be that the funding partners make contributions to different items (for example, parents paying for sheet music and sundries for their own child and LEAs/agencies providing these items for bands, ensembles and orchestras).

In addition, a few respondents mentioned that fundraising was contributing to the costs of equipment, sheet music and sundries, particularly for ensembles and bands. For example, one respondent noted that: 'ensemble music is bought by subscriptions and concert proceeds'. Others mentioned sponsorship and 'friends' organisations as sources of fundraising, providing these items for ensembles and bands.

SUMMARY

The influence of Local Management of Schools and of charging parents for tuition is apparent in several of the findings reported in this chapter. Many providers of instrumental tuition now state that serving their clients is their main purpose. There is a trend towards allocating tuition to schools based on the LMS formula, as well as reacting to demand from parents and schools.

THE ROLE OF INSTRUMENTAL MUSIC

- Over half of the questionnaire respondents stated that the main role of their service, trust or agency was to offer a high quality music tuition service to schools.

- Other roles mentioned were: enhancing classroom music; providing children with experience of music-making; teaching specific skills and developing pupil potential.

- A comparison with data collected in the 1986 NFER survey shows an apparent shift in the perceived role of instrumental music providers: serving the needs of clients (i.e. schools) has become a prominent role.

INSTRUMENTS TAUGHT

- The main orchestral 'families' of instruments (brass, wood-wind and strings) were taught in most LEAs.

- Saxophone, brass band instruments and percussion were taught in more than three-quarters of LEAs.

- The average number of instruments taught ranged from about 15 in the island authorities and Wales, to over 20 in London. There were considerable differences between individual LEAs, ranging from nine to at least 28 different instruments taught.

- A comparison with data collected in 1986 shows a slight decrease in the number of LEAs offering tuition in strings, woodwind and brass (except trombone). The main increases were found in modern instruments (for example, electric/bass guitar, electric keyboards), instruments for the performance of music outside the Western tradition (steel band, sitar, tabla, harmonium) and voice.

- For most instruments, a majority of providing LEAs began tuition in the primary years. Tuition tended to begin in the secondary stage for: saxophone, tuba, bassoon, electric or bass guitar, voice and early instruments. This may be due to the size of these instruments, their expense and their popular appeal for older students.

MUSIC CENTRES

- It is estimated that about two per cent of the total school population in England and Wales attended music centres in 1990/91.

- A total of 483 music centres was reported in 91 LEAs. Three LEAs had no music centre.

- On average, the authorities with the largest number of music centres were English counties and the authorities with the fewest were London boroughs.

- Comparisons with data collected in 1986 show a slight increase in the average number of music centres per authority.

- Youth ensembles, bands and choirs were a feature of music centre activities in all 92 responding LEAs. Over two thirds of LEAs provided for group tuition, choirs, theory and aural work at their music centres.

- A comparison with information collected in 1986 shows an apparent increase in the incidence of choirs and aural work at music centres. It also seems likely that more LEA centres were offering a wider range of music centre activities in 1991 than in 1986.

LEVEL OF PROVISION

- Based on responses received from 69 LEAs, it is estimated that the total number of pupils receiving instrumental tuition in 1990/91 was about 467,500 (between six and seven per cent of the total school population in England and Wales).

- Provision was split fairly evenly between primary and secondary pupils, but only one per cent of special school pupils were estimated to be receiving instrumental tuition in 1990/91.

- Based on responses received from 95 LEAs, it is estimated that approximately 17,000 schools (64 per cent) were receiving regular visits from instrumental service staff in 1990/91.

- On average, secondary schools received the highest level of provision (97 per cent) compared with primary (63 per cent) and special schools (16 per cent).

- Provision to both pupils and schools was lowest, on average, in English counties. This may be due, in part, to the problems presented to services based in those areas, in attempting to reach a large population spread over a wide geographical area.

- Comparisons with data obtained from previous surveys (HMI, NFER) suggest that there has been an increase in the number of pupils, and schools (particularly in the primary sector) receiving instrumental tuition in recent years.

- About a third of respondents to the 1991 survey reported that the average size of instrumental tuition groups had increased in the past five years.

SELECTION

- Over a third of respondents reported that schools were not selected for instrumental provision. These LEAs had adopted a 'fair shares' or 'demand-led' system of allocating teaching time to schools. Other respondents said that their service would be adopting such a strategy in the near future, either giving schools an allocation based on the LMS formula and/or allowing schools or parents to purchase tuition on request.

- The main factors influencing the selection of schools to receive tuition were: historical patterns of provision and the perceived level of support for music in the school. Some LEAs had adopted a policy of targeting the service on 'clusters' or 'pyramids' of schools.

- The selection of pupils to receive tuition was usually a joint decision involving instrumental and school staff.

- A small minority of respondents reported that parents were centrally involved in the selection process, although parents were usually informed once their child had been selected for tuition. In a few LEAs operating agencies or trusts, the final decision rested with parents, who were charged for their child's tuition.

- In LEAs operating pupil selection procedures, musical ability was the main criterion taken into account. This was assessed on the basis of teachers' observations during classroom music and/or by the use of tests and auditions.

- Other attributes considered in selection were the child's interest and enthusiasm for music, and his or her physical suitability for a particular instrument. A small number of respondents said that 'parental support' was also taken into account.

MUSICAL INSTRUMENTS AND EQUIPMENT

- Most LEAs, agencies and trusts were reported to have stocks of instruments available for use by pupils, although these were limited in terms of the number and quality of instruments available.

- These instruments were generally allocated to individual pupils or to schools. In over half of LEAs, instruments were allocated to pupils free of charge for an unlimited period, although in most cases parents were encouraged to buy an instrument for their child, usually after a period of time.

- The repair and maintenance of LEA- or agency-owned instruments was usually the responsibility of the providing body, but schools and parents were expected to contribute towards these costs in just under half of LEAs.

- Responsibility for buying musical equipment (for example, music stands) generally rested with the LEA or agency/trust. The purchase of sheet music and sundries was usually shared between LEA, trust or agency, schools and parents. Fundraising contributed towards the purchase of these items in a small number of LEAs.

4: Management of Provision and Conditions of Employment

Introduction

This chapter looks at some aspects of the management and staffing of instrumental music services, agencies and trusts. The chapter begins by considering management structures and the involvement of LEA advisers/inspectors in the management of instrumental music services. Evidence is presented on posts of special responsibility including those for the coordination of instrumental tuition for children with special educational needs and for tuition of instruments outside the Western tradition.

The issue of quality control in instrumental tuition has become of increasing importance, particularly where instrumental services are facing strong competition from private tutors. The methods used by service/agency managers to ensure quality control are addressed in this chapter. There is also information on the number of pupils taught per FTE member of staff.

A further section focuses on the qualifications, employment conditions and pay of staff. The access of instrumental teachers to in-service opportunities is also addressed, and the chapter ends with a summary of the main points raised in the chapter.

Management and administration

The questionnaire requested information on the administration of instrumental music services. Respondents were asked to list, in order of seniority, the posts of staff involved in running the service. Of the 103 respondents who replied to this, two were unable to give details because their management structures were under review, and one stated that there was, at present, no management structure for instrumental music.

Over a third of those responding to the question described management structures consisting of an LEA inspector/adviser with responsibility for music, a head of instrumental service and a number of other posts such as area coordinators, music centre leaders, heads of instrumental department (e.g. head of strings, woodwind, brass) and other posts of special responsibility.

The second most common pattern, identified in one in five LEAs, was to have an inspector/adviser and several posts of responsibility, with no head of service. Another fairly common pattern (reported in 17 LEAs) was to have a head of service, posts of responsibility but no direct involvement from LEA inspectors/advisers. Ten LEAs reported a smaller management hierarchy with an LEA inspector/adviser and head of service but no other posts of responsibility. Ten LEAs had only an LEA inspector/adviser involved in managing the service, and no other posts of responsibility. Patterns reported in a smaller number of LEAs were: head of service only (two LEAs), area coordinators only (one LEA) and, in one case, the only music teacher was reported to be responsible for class and instrumental teaching on four English islands.

A similar pattern was reported by Cleave and Dust, on the basis of their survey in 1986. However, there is a difference evident in the proportion of respondents reporting a three-tier system (i.e. inspector/

adviser, head of service and other posts of responsibility). In 1985/86 just under half (47 per cent) of LEAs had a three-tier system, whereas in 1990/91 the equivalent proportion of LEAs with such a system was 38 per cent. On the other hand, a management system consisting of a head of service and other posts of responsibility was reported in nine per cent of LEAs in 1986, whereas this pattern was reported in 17 per cent of LEAs in 1991. It is difficult to know whether such differences between the surveys result from differences in the two samples. It is possible, however, that there are fewer LEAs with direct inspector/adviser involvement in instrumental music services in 1991 when compared with 1986. (This point is dealt with in more detail below.)

Administration in Inner London

In 1990 the former Inner London Education Authority was replaced by thirteen separate inner London authorities, ten of which responded to this part of the NFER survey. It was evident from their responses that administration structures were minimal for instrumental music in these small authorities, and were virtually non-existent in some. In six cases, instrumental music was the main responsibility of an inspector/adviser or arts coordinator who organised the service in conjunction with schools. As one inspector (who was responsible for music in two inner London authorities) explained: 'There is no central service as such. As inspector for music, I hold lists of teachers, and schools contact me when they have a vacancy. I send them relevant details and they make their own appointments.' In the four other cases, the system was administered entirely by the schools. However, the Centre for Young Musicians (CYM) offered some additional central coordination for music centre activities in central London. (The organisation of the CYM is discussed in more detail in Chapter 6).

LEA inspector/adviser involvement

The involvement of inspectors/advisers with the provision of instrumental music is potentially an important issue if instrumental music tuition is to make a well-coordinated input to classroom music, particularly in preparation for the introduction of music as a foundation subject in the National Curriculum.

Respondents to the 1991 survey were asked, in a separate question, to indicate whether the LEA music adviser/inspector was the line manager of the instrumental music service. One hundred respondents answered this question, of whom 70 reported that an inspector/ adviser with responsibility for music was directly responsible for instrumental music in their authorities.

In nine cases, the inspector/adviser was also the designated head of instrumental services. Eight large English and Welsh counties had two inspectors/advisers involved in the management of instrumental music, either having a senior music adviser and music adviser or an adviser/inspector for performing arts who had overall responsibility, and a music adviser who oversaw the instrumental music service. In addition, 13 LEAs mentioned the involvement of advisory teachers, as head of service and/or as holders of posts of responsibility within the administration of instrumental music services.

Posts of responsibility

Most LEA services, trusts and agencies had a number of posts of responsibility, often organised on an area basis or in terms of responsibility for the main instrument groups. The English counties tended to have the greatest numbers of such posts, usually organised on an area basis, reflecting the large geographical areas covered by peripatetic services in these authorities. In addition, some had other posts of responsibility, for example, resource management, training coordination, director of youth orchestra or choir and coordinator for school music education (often specifically for music in primary schools).

Twenty LEAs were reported to have a coordinator for provision of tuition for instruments outside the Western tradition. Such posts were most common in metropolitan districts and London boroughs. A similar number of authorities had a member of the instrumental team who was responsible for provision for children with special educational needs. Of the 23 LEAs reporting such a post of responsibility, four were in London boroughs, six were in English and Welsh counties, and nine were in metropolitan districts. One respondent from a metropolitan district reported that the special needs coordinator's post had been 'lost with the voluntary severance scheme' due to cuts in the instrumental music budget. Another adviser in an English county expressed the hope that posts for both 'non-Western' instrumental provision and provision for children with special educational needs would be created when a new agency came into operation in September 1991.

The existence of posts of responsibility for special schools, within instrumental services, appears to have increased since 1986. Cleave and Dust reported that only nine per cent of LEAs had such posts, compared with 21 per cent in 1991. Posts for the coordination of music outside the Western tradition were at around the same level in 1991 as in 1986, when Cleave and Dust reported that about 20 per cent of LEAs had a coordinator for 'ethnic' instrumental music (compared with 19 per cent in 1991).

Quality control

Quality control has become a popular concept within education and many LEAs now have 'quality control' or 'quality assurance' units comprising groups of advisory and inspectorial staff. Managers of peripatetic instrumental services are becoming increasingly aware of the need to monitor the quality of instrumental tuition offered by their staff, a concern which was evident in their responses to the question about the role of instrumental music services (see Chapter 3).

The questionnaire asked respondents to describe the mechanisms existing in their LEAs for monitoring the quality of instrumental tuition. Most of the 103 respondents who replied to this question gave details of both who was responsible for quality control and a number of methods they used to monitor the quality of tuition offered. A small number (13 respondents) said that no such mechanisms currently existed, although three said that steps were being taken to bring in monitoring systems in the near future.

Who is responsible for quality control?

Three-quarters of the respondents said that quality control was the responsibility of service managers and/or LEA inspectors/advisers. In larger LEAs, this was likely to be carried out by area coordinators whereas in a small London borough the music inspector, who was also head of music services, reported: 'We are a small LEA and it is possible for me to develop close working relationships with **all** my staff'. Monitoring quality tended to be the main responsibility of senior music service/agency staff, some of whom had a proportion of time set aside for this purpose. For example, in one large English county the area-based instrumental team leaders spent 26 per cent of their time in liaison with schools, each overseeing the work of the music service in approximately 40 schools.

The inspector/adviser responsible for music education was reported to be involved in quality control in just under half of LEAs. In smaller LEAs (especially inner London authorities) the inspector/adviser was solely responsible for this task.

A number of types of inspector/adviser involvement were reported. In some cases, general inspections of schools usually included an inspection of the peripatetic music staff working at the school. In others, inspectors/advisers were called in by music staff to discuss particular aspects of the service or to deal with specific problems. One respondent from a Welsh LEA explained that instrumental tutors were occasionally interviewed by advisers about the quality of their work. Another respondent from a metropolitan district reported that LEA inspectors were carrying out 'a rolling programme of inspection based on the principle of validated self-review'. In a handful of LEAs specific inspections of music centres or reviews of the whole service were reported. These tended to be in-depth reviews of the instrumental service, resulting in reports containing recommendations for future practice. They were not usually carried out more than once every few years, although one London borough reported a recent major inspection resulting in new guidelines, followed by a programme of regular annual reviews involving discussions on progress between the inspector and the head of service.

At the time of writing, the Government had just announced its plans for a Parents' Charter, which include a number of proposals for the inspection of schools (GB, DES 1991d). While it is not yet clear what implications this will have for LEA inspectors and advisers, it seems likely that their role will change, and that the ability of instrumental services to involve music inspectors/advisers may decline in future.

Monitoring strategies

A number of monitoring strategies were adopted by the music services themselves. It was fairly common for service or agency managers to visit schools to observe lessons taught by peripatetic staff. Fifteen per cent of respondents also reported that some form of appraisal system had been adopted for instrumental teachers, often involving observation of teaching by service managers, report forms completed by instrumental staff and an annual meeting to review each member of staff's work and training needs.

Appraisal

In July 1991 the Department of Education and Science issued Circular 12/91, providing guidance on school teacher appraisal (GB, DES, 1991c). The circular specified that the appraisal regulations, which came into effect in September 1991, do not apply to certain teachers including 'advisory and specialist/peripatetic teachers'. It goes on to point out that 'those responsible for managing such teachers may wish to consider how far appraisal arrangements comparable with those which apply to teachers within the scope of the Regulations can be applied to them (i.e. the excluded staff) unless that would duplicate other arrangements'.

This announcement was greeted with disappointment from some respondents to the questionnaire. As one said: 'We hope to phase in self-evaluation as part of appraisal. This is not required for instrumental staff (but it should be!)'.

School feedback

Feedback from schools was considered an important element by some respondents. In a few cases, school feedback was invited on an informal basis, but some LEAs had instituted more formal strategies for collecting comments from schools. These strategies included: a monthly diary completed by school heads and sent to heads of music centres, questionnaires sent to schools by the service and school record keeping copied to service managers. Some respondents in inner London stated that quality control was mainly the responsibility of schools because, as noted previously, the school heads decided which instrumental teachers to employ: 'schools monitor their own provision and increasingly get instrumental tutors themselves to record and monitor their own work'. One inspector regarded such a system with some concern, saying: 'clearer guidelines are needed and instrumental teachers need to be brought more into the school quality control mechanisms'. In another inner London authority the inspector reported that plans were in hand to improve matters: 'we plan to implement a Borough pastoral scheme for music offering support and guidance to pupils and parents. As part of the scheme, we will encourage all tutors to participate in a pupil assessment scheme, through which clusters of schools will be able to monitor the quality of tuition within their cluster'.

Pupil progress

The collation of information on pupil progress was a popular method of evaluation. Some LEAs instituted their own internal testing system, often combining this with information on results in national music examinations. Some also used information from pupils' school profiles or Records of Achievement as evidence of the standards achieved in music by pupils taught by instrumental staff. Another indicator of progress, reported in a small minority of LEAs, was a check on the number of students dropping out of instrumental lessons.

A few respondents expressed the view that the quality of teaching was best reflected in the standards achieved by pupils in musical performances. As one respondent explained: 'a bad performance would be commented on'. Another described a more formal process whereby an 'event appraisal' was carried out on student performances by the director or deputy of the service.

Recruitment and induction of staff

A matter of comment for a small minority of respondents, was that of the recruitment and induction of new members of staff. Auditions and interviews carried out by instrumental service managers were held to be important in quality control, as were induction schemes (including tailored INSET programmes) and probationary periods for new staff.

Making use of the information

Many LEAs reported the use of a combination of methods, the results of which were discussed at regular (often weekly) staff meetings and contributed towards an internal process of review. In one metropolitan district a new management committee had recently been set up for this purpose, comprising representatives from staff, parents, the LEA, and student observers. Another LEA had taken the unusual step of obtaining external funding for an evaluator to review the work of a strings teaching scheme.

Most of the responses to this question exhibited a concern for instituting effective methods of quality control, and a number of respondents reported that such methods were currently under review. Some made the point that, although quality of tuition was monitored for their staff, there was no equivalent system of monitoring for private music teachers working in schools.

The survey information has shown that many instrumental services are adopting a number of methods to ensure the quality of their service. Some of these methods concern staffing policies (recruitment, induction, training and appraisal), others require the collation of information on pupils (examination results, drop out rates) and liaison with schools. It would seem that the service managers who do not already do so, could benefit from using a combination of such methods in order to set targets and to review progress regularly at meetings with their staff.

Staff–pupil ratios

In Chapters 2 and 3, information has been presented on the number of FTE teaching staff employed by instrumental services and on the number of pupils taught. These two sets of information can be used together, to provide a measure of the number of pupils per FTE teacher for each responding LEA.

Sixty-four LEAs (59 per cent) gave information on both FTE staff and the numbers of pupils taught in 1991. It should be pointed out that in many cases one or both of these figures were estimates, and that the pupil numbers were calculated from percentages of the pupil population served in each authority. Therefore, the figures reported here must be regarded as estimates rather than exact figures.

In order to provide some indication of the 'average' pupil–teacher ratio for instrumental tuition it was decided to report the **median** as opposed to the **mean** (an average derived from adding up the answers and dividing by the number of responses). For skewed distributions, such as the one resulting from these survey data, the median value is a better measure than the mean. (The median is the number which lies in the middle of a set of data, when arranged in order of magnitude.)

The median for the number of pupils taught per FTE member of instrumental staff was 113.1. The estimated number of children taught per FTE teacher varied considerably among LEAs, from 25.7 in one English county to 371.7 in a metropolitan district. Assuming that instrumental staff work a 35 hour week, this would mean that, in the LEA with fewest pupils per teacher, each teacher taught less than one pupil per hour, compared with nearly 11 pupils per hour in the LEA with the highest pupil–teacher ratio.

Such large variations between LEAs are due, in part, to factors which may be outside the control of instrumental service managers (such as the geographical area covered by peripatetic staff, the number of schools served, the type of instruments taught, and the length of lessons). Another factor is the LEA's policy on individual and group tuition, which is, in some cases, influenced by the legislation on charging for school activities (because LEAs charging for tuition generally teach only one pupil at a time). However, the survey data indicated that there was a considerable variation between authorities of the same type and among those adopting the same policy towards group (as opposed to individual) teaching strategies. Although it may not be considered either practical or desirable for staff in all LEAs to teach 11 pupils per hour, it may be worthwhile for all instrumental service managers to collate precise information on pupil–teacher ratios and to use this as a basis to review their organisational, staffing and grouping practices.

Qualifications of teaching staff

The research sought information on the total number of teaching staff employed, and on the training of these staff in relation to both music and teaching qualifications. From the answers to these questions it was possible to calculate the proportion of teaching staff with such qualifications in each authority. Ninety per cent of respondents gave details of the number of both full-and part-time teaching staff they employed, amounting to a total of 5,277 people. Eighty-four per cent of respondents answered the question asking for the number of staff with qualified teacher status (QTS). A few respondents were unsure of the precise numbers, so they gave estimates. From this information it was possible to calculate that, on average, just over half the total instrumental teaching staff employed in these authorities had qualified teacher status. As might be expected, this proportion varied considerably among LEAs, with five reporting that all their teaching staff had QTS, while, at the other extreme, one inspector from a London borough reported that only one member of staff out of 37 held such a qualification.

Seventy-two per cent of respondents gave information about the number of their staff with music diplomas or degrees from recognised Institutions of Higher Education (again, in a few cases these were estimations). On average, over three-quarters of the total number of instrumental staff members were calculated to have such music qualifications. Eight respondents reported that all their staff had music degrees or diplomas. The lowest proportion of musically qualified staff was reported in a London borough, where only 22 out of 128 (17 per cent) held such a qualification.

Part-time staff

Ninety-five respondents gave the total number of part-time instrumental staff employed in their LEAs. There was a relatively high proportion of part-time staff employed in these authorities, amounting to nearly 60 per cent of the total instrumental staff. Again, there was a wide range in the proportion of part-time staff employed, from all the teaching staff in four LEAs to none at all in two authorities.

When asked whether part-time staff were paid a salary or on an hourly rate, 97 respondents replied. Their responses revealed a fairly even split between: salaried (35 per cent), hourly paid (27 per cent) and some salaried, some hourly (38 per cent). Two respondents reported that all, instead of some, of their part-time staff would be paid a salary from September 1991. In 1986, the proportions were somewhat different: salaried (less than 25 per cent), hourly paid (over 50 per cent). Comparisons between the two sets of data would indicate that there has been a shift towards paying part-time staff a salary rather than on an hourly basis, since the previous survey was carried out.

Respondents from LEAs, trusts and agencies employing hourly-paid staff were asked to state the rate of pay per hour. Forty-nine responses were received, representing a range of different types of LEA. The average rate of pay offered in these LEAs was £12.73 per hour. Many respondents point out that rates varied according to the qualifications and experience of the teacher. In one case, different rates were paid according to the age-range of pupils taught and, in another, pay was higher for teaching taking place outside school hours. The amounts quoted varied considerably between LEAs. The lowest quoted figure was £7.54 per hour for unqualified staff working in a metropolitan district. The top rate quoted for qualified staff was £18.88 in an inner London authority. Rates tended to be highest in metropolitan districts and in the London area, and some respondents stated that additional allowances were paid to staff working in large cities. The other type of LEA with higher rates of pay were the island authorities, which offered £16.00 per hour on average to their part-time staff.

Information on recommended rates of pay was obtained from the Musicians' Union (MU) and the Incorporated Society of Musicians (ISM), which agrees recommendations on pay with the Music Masters' and Mistresses' Association (MMMA). The Musicians' Union recommended a rate of £14.00 per hour for private music teachers from September 1991. The ISM and MMMA recommended a range of hourly rates in 1990/91. These rates were specifically aimed at 'visiting instrumental and singing teachers in maintained and independent schools'. Their recommended minimum of £10.30 was for teachers with up to five years' experience, and the top rate was a minimum of £15.31 for teachers with over ten years' experience.

In comparison with the rates recommended by the music teachers' associations, the average rate of £12.73 reported in the survey appears low. However, a few points should be borne in mind. The rate quoted by the Musicians' Union is for 1991/92 (the academic year following the survey) and is for private tutors, who would charge by the hour of contact time. On the other hand, hourly pay for instrumental teachers is likely to include some allocation for preparation and travel. Therefore the hourly rate of pay for instrumental staff is likely to be lower than the private tutors' hourly charge for instrumental tuition. The average hourly rate obtained in the survey is close to that recommended by the ISM/MMMA for teachers with five to ten years' experience. It should also be noted that some instrumental teacher employers offered a salary, rather than an hourly rate, to their more highly experienced and better qualified part-time teaching staff.

Job descriptions

When asked if they provided written job descriptions for their staff, just under three-quarters of the 101 respondents who answered said they provided these for full-time staff. Fewer people responded to the question concerning part-time staff (not all respondents employed part-time staff). Of the 94 who answered the question, half said they provided job descriptions for part-time staff, and a number said they would do so in the near future. The position has changed quite considerably since 1986, when Cleave and Dust found that fewer than a third of the LEAs responding to their survey provided a job description for part-time staff and under half provided job descriptions for their full-time staff.

In-service training

Almost all (91 per cent) of the LEAs, trusts and agencies included in the survey provided some form of in-service training for their instrumental staff. Only five respondents said that there was no such provision. One inspector from an inner London authority explained that the instrumental staff in his area had no in-service provision as part of their contracts: 'A few have come on general INSET courses, but no INSET has been designed specifically for them'. The proportion of LEAs offering in-service training for their peripatetic instrumental staff appears to have increased slightly since 1986, when 85 per cent of LEAs provided INSET for such staff.

It was most common for INSET courses to be organised specifically for instrumental staff and in some cases these were designed for particular instrumental groups (e.g. strings, brass). Over two-thirds of respondents said their staff had access to courses designed for both instrumental teachers and classroom teachers.

Some respondents reported that instrumental teachers were entitled to the same amount of in-service time as classroom teachers, i.e. five training days each year and access to money for further training under the national Grants for Education Support and Training (GEST) scheme. In most cases the training courses were designed and run by music inspectors/advisers and heads of service or other instrumental service managers. A few respondents mentioned that their staff attended courses held at local Institutes of Higher Education. Others said they invited national speakers to make presentations for their instrumental staff. Some LEAs also enabled their instrumental teachers to attend regional or national courses. These courses were often organised by specialist music organisations such as the British Association for Symphonic Bands and Wind Ensembles(BASBWE), the European String Teachers' Association (ESTA) and the Suzuki Institute. One music adviser sent details of a regional course organised by the Music Advisers' National Association (MANA). The aim of the course was: 'to give every support to the staff of our Music services, assisting them to respond to the new challenges'. The course included elements on: teaching styles; the use of language in instrumental lessons; the relationship between instrumental teaching and a child's aesthetic development; and methods for involving pupils in planning and assessing their own learning.

Summary

This chapter has focused on some aspects of the management of instrumental provision and the conditions of employment of instrumental staff.

MANAGEMENT STRUCTURES

- The most common management structure comprised an inspector or adviser with responsibility for music, a head of service (trust, or agency) and a number of other posts of responsibility (e.g. area coordinators, heads of department).

- The LEA adviser/inspector with responsibility for music was the line manager for the service in sixty-five per cent of authorities, and was the designated head of the instrumental service in eight per cent.

- About one in five instrumental services had a coordinator for tuition on instruments outside the Western tradition. A similar proportion had a member of staff coordinating provision for children with special educational needs. These posts were most common in metropolitan districts.

- There appears to have been an increase in posts of responsibility for tuition in special schools since 1986, whereas 'non-Western' music coordinator posts were reported by about the same proportion of LEAs in the two surveys.

QUALIFICATIONS OF TEACHING STAFF

- About half the total instrumental teaching staff in 94 LEAs had qualified teacher status.

- Over three-quarters of the total instrumental staff in 78 LEAs had music degrees or diplomas from recognised institutions of Higher Education.

- The proportion of qualified staff employed by individual LEAs varied widely.

- About three-quarters of respondents provided written job descriptions for full-time staff. This compares with under half of the authorities in the 1986 study.

QUALITY CONTROL

- Most respondents reported that they used methods to ensure the delivery of a high quality teaching service in schools.

- Quality control was most commonly the responsibility of service managers and/or LEA inspectors/advisers, some of whom had a proportion of their time set aside for this purpose.

- Common methods of monitoring quality included: observation of instrumental lessons, appraisal of instrumental staff, feedback from schools and a check on pupil progress.

PUPIL–TEACHER RATIOS

- The estimated average (median) number of pupils taught per FTE staff member was 113.1.

- The estimated number of pupils taught per teacher varied considerably, from 25.7 in an English county to 371.7 in a metropolitan district.

PART-TIME STAFF

- There was a relatively high proportion of part-time instrumental staff employed in 95 LEAs, amounting to nearly 60 per cent overall.

- Music services adopted a mixture of approaches to the pay of part-time staff. Some (35 per cent) paid these staff a salary, some (27 per cent) paid an hourly rate and the remaining 38 per cent paid some part-time staff a salary and others on an hourly basis.

- The average hourly rate of pay in 47 LEAs was £12.73. The lowest rate was £7.54 for unqualified staff; the highest rate was £18.88 for qualified staff in inner London. Hourly pay tended to be higher in the London area, and in metropolitan and island authorities.

- Half the 94 responding LEAs, trusts and agencies provided written job descriptions for their part-time staff. This compares with fewer than a third of LEAs in 1986.

IN-SERVICE TRAINING

- Almost all music service employers provided in-service training opportunities for their instrumental staff.

- In some cases, instrumental staff had the same in-service training opportunities as school staff.

- Training courses were generally provided in-house, although some were run in partnership with local Institutions of Higher Education. Some LEAs funded their instrumental staff to attend regional or national conferences and courses.

5 THE EFFECTS OF THE EDUCATION REFORM ACT ON INSTRUMENTAL MUSIC SERVICES

Introduction

Music service staff are experiencing a period of rapid change, due in part to the provisions of legislation passed in 1988. This chapter presents survey information concerning the main effects of the 1988 Education Reform Act on instrumental music services. Three key aspects are addressed in detail: the effects of the legislation regarding charging for school activities, the delegation of centrally-held LEA funds to schools, and the introduction of a National Curriculum.

The chapter also notes that other changes, particularly in relation to the finance of local government and the oversight of schools by LEAs, may have significant effects on the future provision of instrumental music tuition. An outline of a possible funding scenario is presented, which some music educators believe would offer a degree of stability for instrumental music provision in future. The chapter ends with a summary of the main points to emerge from the data.

Charging for school activities

The 1988 Education Reform Act contained provisions allowing charges to be made for a limited number of activities taking place within or outside normal school hours. This legislation was, in part, prompted by a judgement in 1981 on the legality of levying charges for instrumental tuition. Parents in Hereford and Worcester brought a test case, questioning the authority's right to charge for such tuition. The judge ruled that fees should not be imposed for activities which took place in schools, within the normal school day.

This judgement had widespread effects on instrumental music services. Cleave and Dust reported that, in 1986, services in the 30 LEAs responding to their questionnaire had been affected in some way. The main effects were: the reinstatement of free tuition; requests to parents for voluntary contributions; reductions in the teaching force and range of instruments taught; a transfer of tuition from schools to music centres where tuition could legitimately be charged for out of school hours; and a postponement of plans to begin charging.

The 1988 Education Reform Act upheld the principle of free school education, which had been established in the Education Act of 1944. This meant that activities which were part of the school curriculum, and took place during the school day should be free. One specific exception relating to music education was: 'individual tuition in playing a musical instrument' (subsection 3).

In January 1989, the DES issued a circular (2/89) giving guidance on the interpretation of the legislation regarding charging for school activities. In relation to instrumental music, the circular made the following points:

- Charging is not permitted for class or group musical activities within school hours.

- Music tuition (whether group or individual, inside or outside school hours) must be free if it forms part of the syllabus for a prescribed public examination or is required by the National Curriculum.

- Where the law requires music tuition to be free, parents cannot be required to purchase or hire instruments, to pay for insurance of instruments or to provide sheet music.

- A discretionary charge may be made for individual musical tuition as long as it meets the conditions stipulated above.

- Discretionary charges for individual tuition can cover the cost of the teacher, the cost of sheet music, and the hire and insurance of a musical instrument. Parental agreement must be obtained before pupils are given such tuition.

- There is no obligation on the LEA or school governing body to provide individual instrumental tuition.

- LEAs and schools may ask parents to make a voluntary contribution towards the costs of visits and activities.

- The Act refers to 'tuition in playing a musical instrument'. Its provisions regarding individual tuition do not extend to vocal tuition as the voice is not considered to be an 'instrument'. Therefore individual and group vocal tuition given within school hours must be free. Tuition for singing, provided outside school hours (and not part of a prescribed examination syllabus or the National Curriculum) may be subject to a fee.

- An organisation other than an LEA or governing body may arrange activities to take place during school hours. The third party is able to make charges for these services directly to parents. The LEA or governing body must not take part in such transactions.

In spring 1990, the DES commissioned the NFER to carry out a survey of the provision of school visits and activities and of policies for charging for them (Maychell, K. et al., 1991). The response to the headteacher questionnaire was low, so caution must be exercised in interpreting the results. The authors conclude that there was little overall change in the provision of instrumental music tuition before and after the introduction of the legislation in 1989. However there was a slight, and statistically significant, increase in the number of secondary schools providing individual instrumental tuition between the spring terms of 1989 and 1990. Another statistically significant finding was that parental contributions towards the cost of instrumental music tuition in primary and secondary schools had fallen between the two years. These findings suggest that there was a decline in the number of parents who were willing to make a contribution towards the cost of their child's tuition, immediately following the implementation of the legislation. Some secondary schools appeared to have increased the level of individual provision in order to charge parents a fee for tuition.

The findings of the 1991 instrumental music survey on the effects of the charging legislation

The 1991 instrumental music questionnaire asked: 'What (if any) have been the main effects of the legislation regarding charging for school activities on the provision of music tuition in your LEA?' Ninety-eight people replied to this question, of whom 58 said their provision had **not** been affected. The main reason given by respondents for this lack of effect was that many authorities did not charge parents as a matter of LEA policy. On the other hand, three respondents said they were not affected because they had a long established practice of charging parents for tuition, pre-dating the 1981 judgement. Therefore, in these cases, the reintroduction of the right to charge for some tuition had simply restored the position of a few years previously.

Just under a third of respondents reported that charges had been introduced (or reintroduced) in response to the legislation and, in addition, seven respondents said that their authorities were actively considering introducing charges for instrumental tuition in the near future.

The main elements for which charges were made were: individual tuition, music centre activities held out of school hours, and provision organised by a 'third party' such as a trust or agency.

Charges for tuition in schools

Twenty respondents reported that some parental charges were made in their authorities for individual tuition taking place during the school day. In six authorities, the decision to levy charges for individual tuition was made by the school. These were authorities in which schools had received money or teaching time representing their 'share' of a central instrumental teaching budget. School heads and governors could decide whether to pass on the costs of tuition to parents, or to buy in extra tuition by charging fees. For example, one adviser explained: 'We now charge £13.50 per term for a lesson of about 15 to 20 minute lessons. This charge is made to schools who themselves are responsible for charging pupils (or not as they see fit)'.

The remaining 14 LEAs had policies on charging which were implemented throughout the authority. In three cases, some free tuition was available, but charges were introduced for anything above a certain level of provision or after a certain period of tuition. For example, in one authority, the policy was to allow free tuition on one instrument only. Tuition on a second or subsequent instrument was liable to a charge.

A second authority allowed one year's free tuition whereas in a third, tuition was free for primary school pupils but charged for in the secondary years. The music inspector from this latter authority commented that the policy on charging had affected the continuity of tuition, because about 25 per cent of pupils stopped taking lessons on transfer to secondary school. There were few students studying music at a high level (for example, to Grade VIII) and it had become difficult to sustain central orchestras and bands. Although the council had agreed in principle to abolish fees 'when finance allows' the inspector for music could not foresee this happening in the current financial climate.

Music centre charges

Music centre activities were subject to fees in six cases. These were mainly for lessons on Saturdays and in the evening. Two of these respondents also said parents were required to pay for transport to take their children to and from the music centres.

Charges for group and individual tuition

Following the introduction of the legislation, some LEAs had changed from group to individual tuition so that charges could legally be made. One music inspector questioned the policy of individual tuition in his LEA on educational grounds: 'We have set up a system of individual tuition which is arguably less effective in the early years of tuition than small groups - but we can charge for individual tuition'. Another respondent said 'The inability to charge for group or shared tuition in school time is a major constraint and one that needs urgent addressing by Government'.

Defining 'individual' tuition

The survey revealed some confusion over the precise definition of individual tuition. Tuition in some authorities was provided to small groups of children, and parents were charged for tuition on the basis that each child received individual attention within the group. Two service providers had taken legal advice on this point, with opposite results. One of the respondents explained: 'Since the 1988 Act most of our teaching has been given individually in order to make it legal to levy charges. The latest advice is that "individual" has no legal definition and may not **have** to be coterminous with "singly". We may return to some form of small group tuition for certain purposes.' The other said that the legislation had caused 'confusion' on this point, and added: 'Legal opinion suggests that individual tuition cannot embrace an element of individual tuition within a group i.e. it has to be strictly one to one'. It seems that the definition of 'individual' tuition will not be fully clarified until the interpretation of the legislation is tested in a court of law.

Vocal tuition

Some respondents commented on the effects of the legislation on particular aspects of instrumental music provision. For example, the exception of individual vocal tuition from charges was deemed 'unhelpful' by one respondent who said that this had put the vocal department in his authority 'at a disadvantage'. Another adviser commented that opportunities for vocal tuition in her authority had been 'limited' by the legislation.

Hire schemes

Two respondents reported an impact on their instrumental hire schemes, because it was not now legal to charge for the use of instruments if the lessons themselves had to be provided free. In both cases the money raised by the hire of instruments had been curtailed: one LEA had changed to a 'loan' service, the other had adopted a policy of asking parents to make a voluntary contribution towards the costs of maintenance and repair.

Pupil numbers

The legislation was reported to have had different effects on the numbers of pupils learning. Two respondents said that the implementation (or expansion) of charging following the 1988 Act had enabled them to increase their provision. (Both respondents also commented that the introduction of charges had led to a greater commitment on behalf of parents to their child's tuition.) In another LEA, the introduction of charges had enabled the service to be maintained at its present level, despite a £140,000 cut to its budget. On the other hand, two respondents said that the introduction of charges had led to a reduction in the numbers of pupils learning to play an instrument.

School type and location

In a separate question, respondents were asked whether the charging legislation had had a different impact within their authorities according to school type or location. Sixty-one respondents replied, 49 or whom said there had been no such impact. (In most cases this was because charging was not generally taking place, or because a scheme had been adopted to remit fees for parents facing financial hardship.) Eleven respondents did note differences according to school type or location. The most common pattern was that schools in more 'affluent' areas had a higher proportion of children learning to play an instrument. One adviser commented: 'If parents can afford it they buy an instrument. If not, schools cannot overcome this. There are some LEA instruments but not enough'. Another stated: 'The effect has been essentially socio-economic and rural/urban: 85 per cent of tuition takes place in the South (of the authority), and only 15 per cent in the North, where there are socio-economic problems. Involvement in instrumental tuition becomes dependent on the parents' ability to pay'.

Two respondents predicted that there would be differential effects according to the affluence of the area, if charging were to become widespread in their LEAs: 'It **will** certainly have an impact. Charging should be an "add on", not the main system'.

It seems that the charging legislation has had a variety of effects on the provision of instrumental tuition in about a third of responding

LEAs. A growing number of authorities are likely to introduce charges for this service in the near future, in order to maintain or increase their provision. There is some concern about the effect of charging on the take up of tuition among socially disadvantaged groups. The remission schemes operating in some LEAs help to mitigate such inequalities, but these schemes themselves may be affected by financial constraints. As one Inspector commented: 'We are technically trying to maintain a system which supports free tuition for those on income support. This relies on enough fees being generated. At the moment, the picture looks unbalanced to say the least.'

The impact of the Local Management of Schools on instrumental music services

The 1988 Education Reform Act contained provisions for Local Education Authorities to delegate centrally held funds to schools. The allocations were to be based on a formula worked out by the LEAs and approved by the Secretary of State for Education. Certain elements in an LEA's budget may be excluded from the amount which is available for sharing among schools. This includes capital items, debt charges, funds received from central government and 'such items of expenditure as may be prescribed'. This last category may include central services such as the schools' psychological service, instrumental music and advisory and inspection services. Money which is delegated to schools is not 'earmarked' that is, heads and governors may decide to use money derived from one area of the central budget to fund something else.

The proposals on the Local Management of Schools do not apply to the island authorities of Scilly, Man, Jersey and Guernsey. Inner London authorities will begin delegating their funds to schools in

1992, except for Westminster which had its formula approved and began the process of delegating funds to schools in 1990.

School instrumental music support is one service which many LEAs have sought to keep as a centrally funded item. In April 1989, the Incorporated Society of Musicians carried out a survey of LEA intentions regarding instrumental music. They received 65 replies, of which 52 were proposing that instrumental music should be an 'excepted' service i.e that it should continue to be funded centrally.

More recently, the Government has issued guidelines suggesting that LEAs should delegate at least 85 per cent of their budgets to schools by 1993. In the light of this, more LEAs are now considering the delegation of at least some of the instrumental service budget. This means that future decisions on provision will rest largely with schools, as the final report of the National Curriculum Working Group points out: 'The responsibility for the delivery of the curriculum will in future rest increasingly with governors and headteachers, and we strongly urge every school to have within its general policy a clear statement on its provision for instrumental teaching. Such a statement should define the relationship between instrumental and vocal tuition and class music provision' (GB, DES, 1991b).

The NFER survey, carried out in the summer of 1991, asked respondents to state whether funding for instrumental music had been retained centrally or had been devolved to schools (either partly or wholly). One hundred replies to this question were received, of which 83 indicated that such funding had not yet been devolved. Of the remainder, 13 reported part devolution and four reported that such funds had been wholly devolved.

Respondents reporting partial or total delegation of funding were asked to give further details of the main source(s) of provision for instrumental music. Fifteen respondents replied to this question. The main sources of tuition in these authorities were: from an LEA service (five authorities), private music teachers (four authorities) and schools buying in the services of an agency or music trust (two authorities). Others reported combinations of LEA service, agency/ trust and private tuition.

Ten respondents reported that reviews of the delegation of funding for instrumental music were under way in their authorities or were to be instituted in the near future.

In a separate question, all respondents were asked to give their views on the current and future effects of LMS on their existing instrumental music provision. Most respondents replied to both parts of this question. (The island authorities have been excluded from the analysis because LMS does not apply to them.)

Current effects of LMS

Of the 98 responses to this part of the question, ten were from inner London. These respondents explained that LMS was not yet having any effect in their authorities because the earliest date for delegation was April 1992. Their responses have therefore been excluded from the analysis, giving a total of 88 replies.

In order to obtain an impression of the general reaction towards LMS, responses were put into one of four categories: mainly positive; mainly negative; neutral/mixed; none/don't know. The result of this analysis showed that just over half the respondents felt unable to comment, or said that LMS had yet to affect instrumental music in their areas. In one case, funding for instrumental music had been transferred from the education budget to the Youth Service budget, in order to **prevent** it from being affected by LMS. Of the 43 respondents who could discern an effect, 19 were categorised as neutral or mixed in their opinions, 18 felt the effects had been negative and six reported mainly positive effects of LMS on instrumental music.

Positive effects of LMS

a) *More equitable provision*

The main reported effect of LMS, even in authorities where the funding for instrumental music had not yet been delegated to schools, was to initiate the spread of provision more equitably between schools (see also Chapter 3). As one respondent said: 'The instrumental service is funded from the retained portion of the schools' budgets. Those not receiving peripatetic input are asking why not, since they are paying for it'. Others explained that a redeployment of tuition had already taken place at the request of schools: 'teaching time is being allocated to all schools on a *pro rata* basis. This was implemented at the request of the Head Teachers' Associations'.

b) *Other positive effects*

Three authorities reported an increase in funding and provision due to schools buying more tuition from the service, trust or agency. Other positive effects of LMS reported in one or two LEAs were: a clearer 'targeting' of tuition to meet needs identified by the schools themselves, schools becoming more involved in monitoring the quality of provision, and a raising of the profile of the music service, particularly in relation to its contribution to the music curriculum.

Negative effects of LMS

The two most commonly-mentioned negative effects of LMS were low staff morale and a contraction of the service. Staff morale was reported to be low in several authorities, particularly because of uncertainty about job security. Some respondents also mentioned that they were finding it hard to recruit new instrumental teachers. Two respondents reported that LMS had contributed towards decisions to close down their services entirely. Others said that it had led to a budget cut, resulting in reductions in staffing. In two London boroughs, cuts had resulted in the loss of music advisory teachers. The inspector in one of these LEAs commented that the loss of these advisory teacher posts came at the time when they would be needed most, to help implement National Curriculum music.

Future effects of LMS

Ninety-one responses were received to the question about the likely future effects of LMS on instrumental music. (Responses from inner London authorities are included here, but not those from island authorities, for the reasons given above.) When grouped into the same four general categories, the results were as follows: negative (30), mixed/neutral (27), positive (19), none/don't know (15). It was possible to see some relationships between the geographical location of the LEAs and the type of response given to this question: there was a group of five LEAs in the South of England with positive responses; negative responses came mainly from the North of England and the East Midlands. All of the eight Welsh respondents held strongly negative views.

Negative future effects of LMS

a) Depletion of the service

Fourteen respondents felt that if delegated to schools, their music services would be seriously depleted or would simply cease to exist. One respondent said 'If delegation took place, it (the service) is unlikely to survive because no school would have sufficient funds to purchase staff services'. Respondents predicted that a combination of insufficient school funds and a possible unwillingness among some heads to use their funds to buy music tuition would seriously undermine the viability of a music service in future: 'It is possible that the whole Music Support Service will collapse if schools alone fund the Service'.

b)   *Fragmentation of provision*

Others felt that LMS might lead to a fragmentation of provision, with pupils in some schools receiving tuition and others not. For example, one respondent predicted that schools with a good reputation for music might expand their provision, whilst other, less 'musical' schools would not wish to compete. It was generally felt that larger schools in middle class areas would continue to offer instrumental tuition, in some cases by charging fees to parents. On the other hand, respondents predicted that some schools, especially those in socially disadvantaged areas, small and rural schools, would not be able to sustain the costs of tuition.

Two respondents commented that their current centrally funded system effectively 'protected' schools in rural areas: 'Rural schools find it difficult to find suitably qualified and experienced instrumental teachers within their locality so they are happy for the service to manage the provision'.

The position of small rural schools was of particular concern in large English counties and in Wales. One adviser in an English county said: 'unless more resources are put in the service, small rural schools will suffer because their allocation will be minimal'. The instrumental service in one Welsh authority had put together a document entitled *Music at Risk* arguing against the devolution of instrumental music funding. One of the points made in this document was that the **quality** of tuition in rural schools could suffer because: 'Good tutors would inevitably gravitate toward heavily populated areas, and would not give up earning time to travel to country areas'.

The effect of such disparity was of concern to respondents for two main reasons: first, they objected to the idea that those schools or parents with the most resources should be able to buy tuition, whilst pupils in other schools would have no access to such provision. Second, it was predicted that patchy provision would result in a loss of continuity, particularly when pupils transferred between primary and secondary, or middle and upper schools.

c) Quality of teachers

An area of concern to some respondents was that of quality control: would high calibre staff leave the area in search of better job security; would schools be able to judge the quality of instrumental teachers; would the standard of tuition vary greatly between schools and would schools buy in cheaper private tutors with no guarantee of quality? Two respondents reported that unqualified young people were being asked to give music tuition by schools in their areas. In one case these were students at a local music college; in another, a school had asked its sixth form music students to teach younger children in the school. One respondent predicted a 'gradual erosion of standards of achievement and performance at both school and county level'.

d) Ensembles, bands and orchestras

In a small minority of cases, respondents were worried about the fate of county and area bands, ensembles and orchestras. If all the instrumental music funding were to be devolved to schools, it was felt that school heads and governors would not be prepared to contribute towards the cost of these activities. Even if funding for youth bands and orchestras were to be secured, some respondents predicted that the fragmentation of the service in general, the loss of specialist teachers and a lack of quality control, would eventually lead to their demise.

e) Balance of instruments

A related point, made in a small minority of responses was that the 'balance' of instruments learned may be adversely affected by LMS. Many LEAs effectively control the number of pupils learning different instruments, thus achieving a balance reflecting the composition of a full orchestra or of instruments within wind/ brass bands. (The predominance of tuition on strings, woodwind and brass has already been noted in Chapters 2 and 3). If schools, pupils and parents are able to have free choice, respondents predicted that this may lead to an increased popularity of some instruments and a decline in the tuition of others. Some music educators saw this as a good thing, enabling pupils to chose from a wider range of modern, as well as orchestral, instruments. For others, however, a move away from a Western Classical tradition, and the possible inability to form 'balanced' orchestras, were negative aspects of such a change. As one respondent said: 'the accent on "popular" instruments such as the flute or clarinet (would lead) to unbalanced ensemble experience'.

f)   Other negative effects
Negative points about the effects of LMS made by a handful of respondents were: schools may not be able to afford to repair or replace musical instruments allocated to them from LEA stocks; the ability for instrumental services to support schools in the implementation of National Curriculum music would be diminished; schools would want more classroom support at the expense of practical instrumental tuition; and specialist music courses, currently run by the music service, would disappear.

Positive future effects of LMS

a)   Increase in provision
The main **positive** effect of LMS predicted by our respondents was an increase in instrumental provision due to schools buying in extra tuition from a service, trust or agency. It is difficult to know why these respondents were optimistic about the future when their colleagues in other authorities were predicting that headteachers would not choose to prioritise instrumental tuition over other areas of expenditure. However, some of these responses were from authorities which had set up trusts or agencies, and their managers predicted a positive future for their new ventures.

b)   Meeting local needs
A few respondents commented that LMS would increase the accountability of the existing service and encourage it to meet the needs of individuals and the local community. For example, one inner London authority reported that their existing service was being 'decentralised to seven neighbourhoods and developing service level agreements' with schools. In a large county, the service was being distributed to 'pyramids' of schools which could develop: 'local policies on style, approach,... and a broadening of instruments offered' resulting in 'a considerable increase in community links'.

c)   Other positive effects
Other advantages identified by a handful of respondents were: that schools would value the service more highly if they paid for it themselves; that there could be more opportunities for classroom support; that pupils could chose from a wider range of instruments (see also point e) above); and that provision would be more equitably divided between schools under LMS than at present.

Overview of responses on LMS

It seems that LMS is currently affecting instrumental music provision in about half of the responding LEAs. As noted in Chapter 3, the main effect so far is to spread the service to more schools, particularly primary schools, within each authority. Yet such a redistribution of services without a substantial rise in funding means that some schools will have their existing level of provision reduced in order to provide a service to others. It also follows that the amount of teaching time allocated to small schools may be very little, and that travelling to schools for small amounts of teaching will increase travel and administration costs. This is what Weinburg (1985) has named 'The law of Raspberry Jam', i.e: the wider you spread a resource, the thinner it gets. There are considerable future uncertainties here. Some schools may decide to use the money from the instrumental music budget for some other purpose. If this happens, no child in these schools will have access to tuition unless their parents buy private tuition after school hours. Often schools will wish to satisfy their pupils' demand for music tuition by buying more 'jam' from the supplier (the instrumental service). Some LEAs already operate such a system, allowing schools to buy in as much extra tuition as they wish. One music adviser explained that a two-tier service was operating in his authority, part free to schools and part paid for by schools and/or parents. The central service in this county comprised 62 FTE staff. This was supplemented by a further 40 FTE staff giving paid-for tuition. Schools could decide to receive free tuition only or to supplement their tuition by buying additional teaching time from the music service.

In other authorities there is at present no mechanism for schools to buy extra provision from the music service. As one adviser explained: 'Because of redistribution on an equitable basis, some schools will lose part of the service. A lot will wish to purchase additional teaching to make up the difference. At present there is no mechanism for expanding the service by arranging short-term contracts with schools'. At a recent conference (Willis, K., 1991) some LEA music advisers/inspectors said that local councillors in their areas were opposed in principle to the idea of schools being able to purchase additional tuition. Faced with the inability to buy tuition from the music service, schools may decide to buy in tuition from private music teachers. This may well weaken the position of the existing LEA music services if the funding for music tuition in these areas is eventually devolved to schools.

The role of instrumental music services in supporting the music curriculum

According to the HMI Document *Music from 5 to 16* (GB.DES, 1985) 'much of the success of instrumental work depends on an active partnership being maintained between schools and members of the peripatetic service'. However, such a relationship is not easy to establish or maintain. In their case studies of instrumental services in four LEAs, Cleave and Dust (1989) found that although most of the school staff interviewed felt that 'instrumental teachers should be made to feel part of the school team', some headteachers and music post holders 'admitted they had little contact with their peripatetic staff'.

In their national survey of music advisers and heads of service, Cleave and Dust asked respondents to state what they considered the role of the instrumental teacher should be in relation to class music. The main reaction to this question in 1986 was that instrumental teachers should play a 'supportive and complementary role especially where practical music-making was concerned'. More specifically, respondents suggested that instrumental staff could act as consultants and encourage an appreciation of music by giving demonstrations and recitals to pupils. The authors point out that, despite these views, the teacher union action taking place at the time of their study had affected such liaison and 'There was very little evidence in the case-study authorities of the actual involvement of instrumental teachers in classroom music except where special projects were being tried out'.

The introduction of National Curriculum music in Autumn 1992 will bring about widespread changes to the content of music teaching. It will also have major implications for instrumental service staff, as the final report of the Working Group for music makes clear. In their report (GB.DES,1991b) the Working Group make several references to the potential supportive role which could be adopted by LEA music services. Although the group is careful not to step outside its remit by making suggestions about the delivery of the curriculum, the implication of their report is clear: pupils will need tuition on more than one instrument in order to fulfil the requirements of the National Curriculum. The organisation best suited to help teachers provide such tuition is an instrumental music support service.

In terms of the relationship between instrumental and school staff, the Music Working Group recommends: 'Instrumental teachers should be fully aware of the point their pupils have reached in following the general music curriculum, of the detailed scheme of work involved, and of the tasks and materials used in the classroom. The instrumental music lessons should be regarded as an alternative form of delivery, not as an adjunct or optional extra'.

The 1991 NFER survey of instrumental music providers took place prior to the publication of the final report of the Music Working Group. However, the questionnaire contained a question which was based on the Group's interim report, asking whether respondents felt that their LEA was in a position to further a close relationship between instrumental tuition and classroom music.

Ninety-five respondents replied to this question, of whom 56 were in agreement with the principle of instrumental staff working closely with classroom teachers, and were adopting a variety of strategies to further this aim. Of the remaining 39 respondents, 25 were in favour of the idea of greater integration, but felt there were practical barriers to be overcome, and 13 were opposed to the idea in principle.

Strategies being adopted by service managers to promote a closer relationship between instrumental and classroom staff

The strategies adopted by instrumental managers fell into four main categories: general classroom music support; in-service training; performances, workshops and special projects; and staffing policies.

General classroom music support

Twenty-six respondents said that their staff offered classroom support for music and a further seven had plans to introduce such support. A variety of approaches were adopted, such as working on cross-curricular projects, helping with GCSE and 'A' level preparation, and giving advice to teachers on specific aspects such as improvisation and composition. Some service managers had set up structures to enable this to happen, for example: the appointment of advisory teachers, setting up curriculum support teams and allocating time for peripatetic staff to liaise with classroom teachers. One respondent from an English county explained that a curriculum support team of seven instrumental staff had been formed in 1990. The teachers visited schools once a week to offer support for classroom music, particularly in preparation for the National Curriculum. In September 1991 a second team would be formed to extend this service. The respondent commented that six team members had recently completed a special course on primary school music.

Six respondents mentioned that their peripatetic staff had a proportion of their time earmarked for class support. The amount of time varied from a regular commitment of 10 per cent of the peripatetic teachers' time in three LEAs, to a six-week period out of a 33-week working year, in another. One respondent reported that although curriculum time was currently built into instrumental teachers' timetables, this arrangement would cease shortly at the request of the authority's Education Committee.

In-service training

Many respondents recognised that instrumental staff would need adequate training and preparation if they were to become involved in classroom music education, and about one in five made specific reference to INSET undertaken by their staff. In some cases in-house courses had been designed for this purpose. For example, one LEA service kept Monday afternoons free of instrumental tuition so that the peripatetic staff could meet for in-service work. This included: 'the preparation of topic-based project work' designed by small teams of the staff for use in primary schools. In some cases, the training was designed to help staff adopt a consultancy role. In others, INSET had been based on particular musical approaches, chosen for their applicability to classroom teaching. For example, in-service work on general classroom instrumental teaching based on the approaches of Kodaly and Orff, had been instituted for peripatetic staff in one Welsh authority. The adviser commented: 'This helps them to transfer their skills into more general classroom music'.

Some music services had sent staff on courses at Institutions of Higher and Further Education. In addition to the primary music course run by the Exeter University (mentioned above), instrumental staff in another LEA had attended a primary music consultancy course at Bath College. A short course had been specifically designed for 20 instrumental tutors by LEA staff in a new London authority, and had been validated by Trinity College of Music. (See also Chapter 4 for more information on in-service training.)

Performances, workshops and projects

Another main category of classroom support mentioned by one in seven instrumental service managers, was that of performances, workshops and projects. Many instrumental services had staff bands and ensembles which gave performances to groups of pupils. One county music service had produced a series of booklets for use in schools. The material included information about the staff ensemble which was described in the following terms:

> *With its emphasis on quality in content, presentation and performance, the Ensemble is able to project an atmosphere of enjoyment through music-making and at the same time achieve sound educational objectives by means of live illustration. The group offers a comprehensive service to all schools including special schools, and audience participation forms an integral part of presentation. Work in secondary schools includes 'workshop' sessions on GCSE-related projects, including the performance and analysis of student compositions.*

Workshops and projects were usually run by groups of instrumental staff and tended to be aimed at primary children or at secondary GCSE music students. One music adviser described a series of different types of projects offered by his staff including ones on: folk music, led by the service and class teachers; 'Sounds Exciting' workshops held once every two weeks and 'Strings and Things' - a series of lessons planned for one whole day. Another respondent reported that workshops offered to secondary GCSE groups by his staff aimed to: 'assist students with composition, orchestration, performance, and presentation'.

In some cases, these workshops and projects contained an in-service element for school staff. For example, one LEA ran a series of curriculum support sessions for pupils and teachers. These had the dual purpose of improving pupils' musical skills and of helping the class teacher to 'become more comfortable' in leading similar music sessions. In another authority the music service had developed a school-based in-service course for primary teachers. This cost £1,000 for a one-week course. Other respondents pointed out that they designed INSET courses for class teachers to attend alongside instrumental teaching staff.

In a few cases, respondents mentioned the involvement of professional musicians in music projects run for the benefit of teachers and pupils. For example, an inspector in a London borough reported working with London Sinfonietta and other professional groups to provide composition projects in schools. There was also an example of music staff linking with students on an HE course. An inner London authority had liaised with the Guildhall School of Music and Drama to provide placements for music students. The students were from a Performance and Communication Skills (PCS) course developed by the Guildhall. The music inspector described this as a 'pioneering' development: 'These young musicians work alongside many of the more experienced instrumental teachers and bring welcome and new ideas into the schools. The underlying *raison d'etre* of the PCS course is to improve the style of instrumental teaching and bring it into line with some of the more recent innovations in classroom practice.'

Staffing policies

A few respondents mentioned that they had, or were about to institute staffing policies in order to help their service work more closely with school staff. The most commonly mentioned strategies were: to create posts of responsibility for classroom liaison (for example, advisory teachers, curriculum support coordinators) and to recruit new staff with specific experience and skills. For example, one music adviser stated: 'Our policy has been to employ teachers who have a real grasp of education as a whole - not just instrumental teaching or music education'. Another said 'all recent appointments have been on the basis of good teaching skills, sound philosophy and flexibility'.

Other strategies

In addition to the main strategies outlined above, a small minority of respondents mentioned the use of instrumental service resources by classroom teachers. These included music libraries, the loan of large or unusual instruments to schools (e.g. gamelans), and the development of workpacks and classroom materials by instrumental staff. One LEA had built a new music resource base for use by classroom teachers and instrumental staff. Another had developed a 'sound technology bus' which comprised a mobile electronic music studio. The bus travelled to upper and high schools in the county, and was so successful that another bus had been added for use by middle schools.

Barriers to change

As noted above, a substantial minority of respondents were either opposed to the idea of closer integration between instrumental service and school-based staff, or felt that there were barriers in the way of progress towards this aim. The main concerns raised by these respondents centred on the availability of resources and the role of the instrumental service in relation to classroom music.

Several respondents said that lack of resources would curtail their ability to support classroom music education. In two cases, the service had been disbanded altogether, in others financial constraints were already being felt and heads of service commented that they would be unable to offer support of this kind, unless more resources were made available to them. A second related point made by some respondents was that instrumental teaching should be the main purpose of the service and that this would be adversely affected by the addition of new tasks. As one adviser said: 'The instrumental staff and music staff in schools already have good working relationships... However, to allow time for the instrumental staff to work within the classroom means less time for instrumental teaching. We are unable even now to meet the demand for the service in schools'. Another commented 'If a case can be made for instrumental help in the classroom, then we should fight that case on its own merits, not at the expense of the instrumental service... We should not rob Peter to pay Paul'.

Other respondents explained that their instrumental staff were unable or unwilling to take on the role of classroom support; as one adviser said: 'not all teachers are suitable for this extension to their work'. Another explained: 'If asked to prioritise, the peri's would prefer to teach the committed than spread (themselves) thinly around the classroom with a hazy job spec.' An associated point made by one inspector concerned the status and pay of instrumental staff. He stated that classroom work would only be possible 'if qualified status is considered for instrumental teachers' and added 'at the moment, instructors are being asked to do work with, or for, qualified school-based staff ie INSET etc. However, they are paid as unqualified staff'.

Two respondents said they believed that more involvement by peripatetic staff in the classroom would undermine the resources available to the class teacher. As one pointed out: 'If headteachers saw them (i.e. peripatetic staff) helping within the classroom, it would lead to a reduction in the time that classroom music teachers will be allowed for the teaching of music'. Another respondent said it would be unfair to other subject areas if music were effectively 'double staffed' due to instrumental teachers working in the classroom.

Several respondents from inner London identified organisational difficulties in achieving the aim of closer liaison, due to the fact that the music service in their areas was largely run by individual schools. As one inspector said: 'The service is not centrally managed. Individual schools may well be agents for integration but there is none at the centre'.

A few respondents said that, in their opinion, a move towards classroom teaching by instrumental staff was not desirable because this would undermine the distinctive nature of the service and lay it open to financial cuts. One respondent summed this up by saying 'the more the work of instrumental staff becomes integrated with that of class teachers, the more it is liable for cutting without being noticed. There is an argument for keeping instrumental work specialised because its loss is therefore more noticeable'.

Summary of points on support for music taught in class lessons: some suggestions for a more positive role for the instrumental music service

The points reported above give interesting indications of the kinds of problems which will have to be faced if it is felt desirable for the instrumental service to become more actively involved in the delivery of the school music curriculum. It seems that a majority of respondents were in favour of such a move but that it will need to be handled carefully in order to avoid the instrumental service losing its specialist (and much valued) role.

In some ways, the situation of instrumental teachers is analogous to that of professional artists working in schools (see Sharp, C. and Dust, K. 1990). The aim should be for both 'partners' (i.e the instrumental teacher and the classroom teacher) to share expertise for the benefit of pupils, not for the instrumental teacher to take over the class teacher's role. (In a situation where there is a shortage of music teachers, particularly in secondary schools, there is a danger that headteachers may be tempted to use instrumental staff as supply teachers.) However, seen in the light of a productive partnership, the instrumental service could perhaps best support the class teacher by:

- offering advice on specific aspects of music education (consultancy)

- providing experience of live music-making (performance)

- working alongside teachers on specific projects planned and negotiated between school and instrumental staff (project work)

- sharing expertise with class teachers, given support from advisory staff (INSET)

- providing resources which schools would be unable to purchase for themselves (e.g. access to instruments and music technology)

It is clear that certain criteria will have to be met before these aims can be achieved. First, there must be sufficient resources to enable instrumental services to offer a specialist service as well as classroom support. Second, existing instrumental staff must be willing to take on this role, and training should be provided to help them develop their consultancy and negotiation skills. Third, services will need to recruit new staff with specific skills, although this may be difficult to achieve while there is a shortage of classroom music teachers. Instrumental staff should also be offered rates of pay on a par with class-based staff. Finally, in order to offer a coordinated service, some form of central or regional organisation is required. The comments from the inner London authorities are interesting in this respect, suggesting that coordination is very difficult in a situation where individual schools are responsible for employing instrumental staff. This serves to highlight possible future difficulties in offering to support all the schools in the introduction of National Curriculum music, if LEAs decided to delegate their instrumental service funding to individual schools in future.

Other challenges

Some respondents to the questionnaire raised other issues which they felt would affect the future of their instrumental music services. These concerned timetabling difficulties, the affects of schools opting out of local authority control, and the future of local government in England and Wales.

Timetabling

A few respondents mentioned that they were finding it difficult to arrange instrumental lessons to the satisfaction of schools and parents. (See also the comments from teachers and heads on the timetabling of lessons, in Chapter 6.) It was felt that the introduction of the National Curriculum and the popularity of continuous assessment had increased the pressure on pupils who were absent from lessons. This was of particular concern for older pupils, especially those taking instrumental music lessons in addition to National Curriculum studies at Key Stage 4 (ie for pupils aged 14 to 16). Respondents were reluctant to see the provision for music tuition move outside the school day, because then there would be a danger that instrumental music would be seen as an 'optional extra' rather than as an extension of the music curriculum in schools.

The effect of schools opting out of LEA control

Some respondents were worried about the effect on central services, such as instrumental music, if several schools in the authority were to obtain Grant Maintained Status (GMS) and leave the LEA. The Government has decided that all schools which become grant maintained must be given compensation from the LEA for centrally provided services which the schools have previously received free of charge. This is stipulated as 16 per cent of the GM schools' budgets.

The effect of schools 'opting out' of LEA control is hard to predict. If many schools are granted GMS within an authority where instrumental music is paid for centrally, this is likely to result in a reduction of the music service budget. Depending on the individual circumstances, GM schools may in fact receive a greater amount of compensation than is represented by the costs of providing them with instrumental tuition, thus creating a deficit for the service.

It may therefore be an attractive option for music staff to consider delegating the instrumental service money to schools, thus lessening the overall effect on instrumental service budgets of some schools opting out. On the other hand, LEAs which have delegated around 85 per cent of their budgets to schools are reported to be reluctant to take delegation further (Pyke, N., 1991). This is because any school obtaining GMS will take its own delegated budget plus a disproportionate amount of the dwindling central budget, away from the LEA.

When a school opts out of local government control, there is nothing to stop it buying back services from the LEA, as one of the people interviewed in the research pointed out (see the description of the Kent Music School in Chapter 6). However, the future position remains uncertain, as the music adviser in an English county reported: 'more and more schools are becoming grant maintained. It is not clear exactly how much demand there will be for instrumental teaching provided by the County service for these schools. So far, there have been no redundancies and it looks as though the music service will continue to be centrally funded in the 1992/3 financial year, but no final decision as yet'.

The future of local government

As some respondents noted, if a majority of schools within an LEA become maintained by central government, then the authority will gradually lose funding and control of schools until the LEA eventually ceases to be a viable entity. This would be a slow 'death' for LEAs, but there has been speculation that the present Government may wish to see a more dramatic change, by removing education spending from local government, and placing it under central government control. The effect of such a radical change on non-statutory services, such as instrumental music, is difficult to predict, but without local government funding it is likely that the services provided in many areas would simply cease to exist. This is one reason for service managers exploring the possibility of other forms of organisation for music services (such as trusts and agencies) which would have a chance of survival if such a momentous change in the funding of education were to take place.

The need for central government finance

Some of the participants in this research suggested that central government should provide funding for instrumental services on a national basis in future. As one adviser said: 'LEAs are proving unreliable guardians of the service. A national funding body is needed to grant-aid area music schools.' He went on to suggest that a sort of 'Youth Arts Council' would be an appropriate analogy for such a national body. A number of proposals were being made by music advisers/inspectors and music organisations about how such a scheme could work. The common principles were that a body should be set up to administer grants, possibly on a similar basis to the operation of the scheme for funding in-service training (GEST). LEAs, trusts or agencies could make bids to the funding body for grant aid. The direct grant could be supplemented by other funding sources such as local government grants, sponsorship and income generation (e.g. fees for tuition and courses, box office returns). There would have to be extra central government support available for areas of social deprivation where it would be difficult to raise funding from sponsorship and parental fees. The guidelines for bids could also stipulate that a fee remission scheme should be set up in any area where charges were made for the service. It could also ensure that instrumental service providers would tailor their services to meet the needs of the community, including provision for instrumental tuition outside the Western tradition and support for children with special educational needs.

Those proposing such a system believed that it would have many advantages. It would ensure funding for instrumental services on a national level and would help service managers to develop their existing provision to meet the need for classroom music support. It would secure a basic entitlement to instrumental support for all schools, whilst allowing the freedom for some schools and parents to supplement this if they so wished. A national funding scheme would also ensure that youth bands, choirs and orchestras could continue to survive and thrive.

Summary

This chapter has considered some of the main influences on instrumental provision, arising from the 1988 Education Reform Act, and has outlined both their current and future effects.

CHARGING FOR INSTRUMENTAL TUITION

- Over half of the 98 respondents said instrumental tuition had not been affected by the legislation regarding charging for school activities.

- Just under a third of LEAs had introduced (or re-introduced) charges for tuition following the introduction of the 'charging' legislation. A number of others were reported to be actively considering introducing charges in future.

- There was some confusion over the definition of 'individual' tuition. Some authorities were charging parents for tuition taking place in small groups, on the basis that each child received individual attention within the group. Others had moved from group to individual tuition so that charges could be made.

- Twelve respondents said that charging policies had a differential effect according to school type or location. The most common pattern was for schools in more affluent areas of an authority to have more children learning to play an instrument.

LOCAL MANAGEMENT OF SCHOOLS

- Seventeen LEAs had devolved all or part of their instrumental service budget to schools. The possible delegation of this budget was being reviewed in a further ten authorities.

- Over half of respondents said that LMS was yet to have an effect on their services. A substantial minority reported that LMS had initiated a more equitable spread of music tuition to schools.

- When asked about the likely **future** effects of LMS, just under a third of respondents felt it would have a negative influence. Negative responses were most common in the north and east Midlands and in Wales.

- Predicted negative effects of LMS included: a depletion of the overall budget; an uneven spread of provision, with rural schools and schools in 'deprived' areas losing out; fragmentation of provision; and a complete closure of the service.

- Nineteen respondents predicted positive effects of LMS, including expansion resulting from schools buying extra tuition; increased accountability; and an ability to meet the needs of the local community and of individual schools.

THE ROLE OF
THE INSTRUMENTAL MUSIC SERVICES
IN SUPPORTING THE MUSIC CURRICULUM

- Fifty-six respondents said their services were supportive of classroom music-making. Strategies included: general support of classroom activities; in-service training for school staff; performances, workshops and special projects; and staffing policies (for example, the creation of posts of responsibility for classroom liaison and the recruitment of new staff with particular skills).

- Twenty-five respondents said there were considerable practical barriers to be overcome before closer integration could be achieved, and 13 were opposed to the idea in principle.

- The main concerns of these respondents centred on a tension between the specialist and generalist role for the service. Some respondents pointed out that instrumental staff were unwilling or unable to take on the task of classroom support.

OTHER CHALLENGES

- Some respondents predicted that difficulties of timetabling instrumental tuition, the effects of schools opting out of LEA control and the uncertainty over the future of local government would represent further challenges to instrumental music services.

A POSSIBLE WAY FORWARD

- Some of the participants in this research suggested that central government should provide funding for instrumental services on a national basis in future. This could operate in a similar way to the scheme for funding in-service training. It was believed that such a scheme would help to ensure the future of instrumental music services.

6 MUSIC TRUSTS, AGENCIES AND FOUNDATIONS

Introduction

The purpose of this chapter is to examine alternative forms of funding and organisation of instrumental music services in England and Wales. The main part of the chapter consists of portrayals of five music services which are organised in a variety of ways. Each description is based on interviews and available documentation. The portrayals are necessarily a reflection of the views of the people interviewed. In each case, the text was sent to the participants for amendment and approval, and the consent of the authority was obtained in relation to information supplied by LEA staff.

The chapter uses data from the survey to put these portrayals into a national context. Information drawn from the interviews and the questionnaires is used as a basis for summarising the main disadvantages and advantages of agencies, trusts and foundations.

It is hoped that this chapter will be of interest and use to readers who may wish to consider setting up such a system in their own areas.

The national picture

From the questionnaire responses, it was evident that there was widespread interest in the idea of organising music tuition services as semi-autonomous units within an LEA. Two main types of organisation were proposed: an agency (which could be profit-making) and a trust (or, less commonly, a 'foundation') which would obtain charitable status and operate as a non-profit making organisation.

Although one LEA had established its music trust as long ago as 1948, interest in 'alternative' forms of organisation has evidently grown in recent years. In fact, three LEAs had recently set up music trusts or agencies, and seven respondents reported that such organisations were being formed in their LEAs. Ten respondents said that the possibility of a music agency or trust was being actively considered in their authorities. Of the 21 LEAs which were considering setting up a trust/agency (or had already done so) 11 were English counties, six were in the London area and four were metropolitan districts.

Reasons for the recent interest in agencies, trusts and foundations

The main reason behind the interest in music trusts/agencies was a simple one: LEAs were attempting to preserve their music services and, in some cases, to expand their current level of provision. Respondents were worried that their present services would be vulnerable to cuts caused by lack of central funding and LMS. It was believed that the manager of an agency/trust would be able to make decisions on strategy and act more independently of the LEA.

In most LEAs it was planned that the new service would be supported by a local authority grant and supplemented by fees charged direct to schools and/or to parents. There was particular interest in the possibility of charging fees for tuition. As one respondent explained: 'Over the next five years, the LEA is looking into the possibility of creating a grant-aided charitable trust, supported by the LEA but independent of it. This will enable certain charges to be made in order to supplement and enhance staffing'. (See Chapter 5 for information on the legislation regarding charging for school activities.) In some cases, a dual system was proposed, allowing an agency or trust to operate alongside an LEA service. In such a system, all schools would receive some free tuition from an LEA service (allocated on the basis of the LMS formula). Any school or parent wishing to buy extra instrumental tuition could apply to the trust or agency, and would be charged a fee.

In one authority, an independent agency had been set up by parents in response to the council's decision to cut costs by closing its instrumental teaching service. When the council was faced with the threat of community charge capping it had decided to reduce its expenditure by cutting its funding for the music service. The new agency, which will be administered by area parent groups, will employ some of the 30 music service staff who were made redundant by the council in May 1991. The agency will generate revenue from parental fees, with some additional finance from school budgets. Trust funds have been set up in order to attract external funding to help support children whose parents cannot afford to pay for tuition. The parents' committee has put together an information pack for schools, and hopes to begin operating the agency from September 1991.

This example of a 'private' agency is, however, atypical, although parents in the other LEA which has recently closed its service were also setting up an agency in order to keep a reduced service going by charging fees. In all other cases it was the LEA and music service staff who were primarily responsible for setting up agencies, trusts and foundations.

Alternative forms of organisation - five examples

The following five examples describe different forms of music service organisation in five areas: Kent, East Sussex, Croydon, inner London, and Knowsley. These examples have been chosen to show a variety of possibilities for organising and funding music tuition. Both Kent and East Sussex have music schools which offer tuition to parents on a fee-paying basis. In Croydon, a music agency was established in order to provide a music service to schools. Schools purchase tuition from their delegated school budgets, and some pass on tuition charges to parents. The Foundation for Young Musicians was set up in order to preserve some centrally organised music tuition for central London, after the abolition of the ILEA.

The final example is included by way of contrast to the other four. In Knowsley, the music service forms part of a performing arts service, which has recently suffered a substantial budget cut. The LEA has not decided to pursue the possibility of a trust or agency, preferring to retain a service model. The funding for the service will be delegated to schools in 1992. The service staff and headteachers interviewed foresee that many heads will not be willing or able to buy back the service, thus reducing provision still further. However, it is possible that LMS may bring increased revenue for the service in future.

The Kent Music School

Introduction

The Kent Music School (KMS) is one of the longest established music trusts in England and Wales. In 1929, Mary Ibberson established the Rural Music Schools' Association, with the aim of serving people in rural areas. The Kent Music School was one of 15 rural music schools set up by the Rural Music Schools' Association. The KMS is an independent registered charity. It receives its funding from the local authority and from parental fees. Michael Wearne has worked for the KMS for 21 years and has been its director for 13.

Funding for the KMS

The KMS receives an annual block grant from the local authority which currently represents about 50 per cent of its income (i.e. £1.459 million, out of a projected turnover of approximately £2.9 million for 1991/92). The local authority grant comes from two sources: £959,000 from the education budget 'grants to voluntary organisations' and £500,000 from 'corporate policy provision', a non-education budget which councillors vote to expend on areas of provision of importance to the community within Kent.

It has been agreed that the grant received from the corporate policy provision will be reduced by £500,000 to nil over the next three years. The education budget for 'grants to voluntary organisations' will be increased in line with inflation. Thus, in order to maintain its provision in the context of an overall grant reduction, the KMS will have to adopt a number of strategies for the generation of new income in future.

Organisation, staffing and tuition

The KMS operates from its head office based in Maidstone. There are six area offices, each with an area director and an area head of instrumental teaching. There are 18 music centres, each with a head of centre.

The service employs 265 instrumental staff, most of whom work part-time. Figures provided for the three years from 1989/90 to 1991/92 show a steady increase in the number of full-time equivalent staff employed, from 114.1 in 1989/90 to 120.3 in 1991/92. The staff give tuition on a wide range of instruments including: strings, woodwind, brass, piano/keyboard, recorder and voice. There are currently five FTE posts for general music tuition, i.e. kindermusik, musicianship and theory.

The peripatetic staff visit just over half the 754 schools in Kent on a regular basis. Michael Wearne estimates that approximately seven per cent of the primary population and five per cent of the secondary population are currently receiving tuition from KMS staff. The KMS arranges to visit schools by invitation.

Michael Wearne is anxious not to turn down any school or individual parent requesting music tuition. In order to provide flexible staffing, the KMS interviews and appoints to its 'bank' of teachers private music tutors who operate in schools. Private tutors wishing to be licensed by the Kent County Council are 'vetted' by the County Music Adviser or by the KMS acting as agents to the LEA. Successful applicants are put onto a waiting list until a vacancy in a school becomes available. The licence ensures that the tutor is properly covered by insurance and has achieved a good standard of tuition. The KMS enters into an informal agreement with licensed tutors, and provides them with written advice, including guidance on the level of fees currently charged by the KMS. Some of these licensed teachers will eventually join the KMS teaching force on a permanent basis.

Parental fees

Pupils usually receive a course of 33 instrumental lessons per year. Both individual and group lessons are offered. Charges vary according to the size of group from about £28.50 per term for a series of 40-minute group lessons, to £58.50 per term for 30-minute lessons on an individual basis. The lessons are subsidised by the local authority grants. Michael estimated that for individual lessons (charged at £10.63 per hour) the subsidy amounts to £7.80 per hour. For a group lesson with six or more pupils there is effectively no local authority subsidy because income from fees covers the cost of providing the lesson.

There are two sources of financial help for parents who are unable to afford to pay for their child's instrumental tuition. Parents earning less than £9,000 a year can apply to the Kent County Council for part or full remission of fees, depending on their level of income. The KMS has a bursary fund to help children whose parents earn between £9,000 and about £12,000 a year. Around 400 pupils are currently supported by the County Council and a further 100 have their fees paid by the bursary fund.

The KMS is independent of the LEA and individual schools. It therefore offers its services to parents as a third party, and, as such, is able to charge for tuition under the terms of the legislation regarding charging for school activities.

Music centres, courses and classroom support

The 18 music centres offer a wide variety of musical activities for children and adults. They provide the focus for numerous area ensembles, orchestras and choirs and were attended by approximately 7,000 children in 1990/91. All areas offer a number of evening, weekend and holiday courses for people at different stages of musical development. Parents bringing their children to classes at music centres are offered the chance to learn an instrument themselves. In addition, the KMS liaises with institutions offering adult education to provide music classes for adults.

In terms of classroom support, KMS teachers offer workshops to schools and help children studying for GCSE and 'A' level. All instrumental teachers are required to give lessons for 33 weeks of the 39-week school year. This leaves six weeks for KMS teachers to contribute to work in schools.

Provision to Grant Maintained Schools

Michael Wearne acknowledges that if schools opt out of local authority control, this will deplete the education budget which contributes to the funding for the KMS. For this reason he is keen to provide instrumental tuition to schools which are grant maintained. One such school is the Cornwallis School based in Maidstone, which opted out of the LEA in April 1990. The KMS has negotiated with the school to provide lessons at the true cost (i.e. without the local authority subsidy). The school has arranged to reclaim the difference from the Department of Education and Science so that parents of children at Cornwallis pay the same amount as other parents in the area.

Melinda Carr is Head of Performing Arts at Cornwallis School, which has approximately 850 pupils aged 11 to 17. Pupils receive tuition on clarinet, saxophone, flute, piano and brass instruments. Some pupils also attend classes for violin and other stringed instruments at the local music centre. Melinda feels that the instrumental service makes an important contribution to the school: 'It gives opportunities for children to perform in concerts and they contribute to promoting the school. It enhances group work and gives pupils a discipline for learning. In classroom music, it is a bonus if you have someone who can play a bass line for the class.'

Overall, Melinda is very pleased with the service provided by the KMS. Her only 'bone of contention' is that she does not like group tuition. This is for two main reasons: she feels that after the first term of lessons, pupils begin to progress at different rates and therefore ideally require individual tuition. She also points out that group tuition can cause practical problems, for example, accommodation, noise levels and the need to release several pupils (often from the same lessons) to attend.

Publicity, marketing and quality control

As well as holding demonstrations of music in schools, the area directors regularly visit the heads of schools in their region to promote the services of the KMS. Michael Wearne is keen to open up new areas of provision: for example, the service is now prioritising work with special schools, very few of which currently receive the service. The KMS is exploring new ways of working with children with special educational needs, including the recruitment of instrumental teachers who wish to specialise in this area of work.

In terms of the wider community, the KMS promotes its work through publicity at concerts and courses. It also uses advertising in local newspapers and leaflets to homes. Michael feels that the future of the KMS depends on widespread satisfaction and support for the service. This means that the service will attempt to provide tuition on any instrument for which there is a demand. He sees marketing as an essential part of the job of the instrumental staff: 'Every one of our teachers is a salesman or saleswoman.'

Quality control is a vital element in the success of the KMS. All full-time staff take part in a staff appraisal scheme. The County Music Adviser and the Advisory Teacher for Music monitor the quality of the service on behalf of the LEA. The KMS also operates its own probationary scheme and in-service training programme.

Incentive allowances are offered for full-time staff appointed to take on extra responsibilities.

Looking to the future

Although its main sources of income are local authority grants and parental fees, the KMS is looking to expand its income from parents and other sources, particularly in view of the future reduction in the local authority grant. Strategies include increasing group tuition, introducing differentiated fees according to the 'calibre' (ie the experience and qualifications) of the teacher, expanding the instrument hire scheme and selling instruments to parents.

The KMS has also begun to offer consultancy to other LEAs. This arose because of the number of requests that the KMS received from LEAs for help and advice on how to manage their instrumental provision. While Michael Wearne is happy to discuss these issues over the telephone, the KMS has begun to market its services on a consultancy basis to those who want more detailed advice.

In order to explore the possibilities of longer term commercial sponsorship in Kent, the KMS Board of Governors has recently agreed to engage a consultant to carry out an 'audit' of the service and to draw up an action plan.

Advice to others

Michael Wearne feels that the decisions made by some LEAs substantially to reduce funding for their music services are short-sighted. He feels strongly that the right course of action for all LEAs is to recognise the 'growth-through-earnings potential' of such services by expanding them on a business-like basis and supporting them with short- or medium-term loans until they achieve greater independence. He argues that it is better to raise revenue by charging some parents for the service (and offering bursaries to children whose parents cannot afford to pay) than to try to provide free tuition to some and risk losing the service altogether. He concedes that it is much more difficult in some areas to raise money from fees, but believes that a higher level of local government grant may be necessary to support the service in such areas. Michael Wearne feels that a semi-independent body which raises some money from fees is in a stronger position to continue providing music tuition than a totally LEA subsidised service. He also makes the point that: 'Wherever there is a possibility of private teachers offering their services and charging fees, there is the opportunity for establishing a music school that charges fees but gets a subsidy from the county council.'

The East Sussex Music School

Background

In 1984, East Sussex LEA employed 35 FTE peripatetic music teachers, three advisory music teachers and three teachers who taught on the music preparatory course (for students aged between 16 and 19). There were also two music advisers in the LEA. The peripatetic teachers were only sufficient in number to visit about half of the schools in the county. This pattern of provision was largely historical, dating from before the reorganisation of local government in 1974. The system also favoured schools which, in the view of the music service, were most likely to make good use of the resource. Children were selected by the schools, on the basis of a 'Bentley' test and the teacher's judgement of the child's motivation to learn an instrument.

Establishing a charitable trust

In 1984, the music service was effectively unable to respond to any growth in demand for music tuition. The LEA grant was relatively static (although it was increased annually to keep pace with inflation).

Roger Durston, the County Music Adviser, had had experience of setting up and operating a County Music Trust (in his previous post as Director of the Berkshire County Music Department) at no additional cost to the LEA. There was a music trust already in existence in East Sussex, but this trust had had a very limited role in music education within the county. He therefore worked with the county education officers to explore further possibilities. In 1986 the decision was taken to revive the trust and to expand its role to develop Saturday morning and weekday evening music centres in five areas of the county. The LEA and county music staff agreed a pattern of flexi-time working which, they believed, would ensure the best value for money was obtained from the staffing budget, while providing an opportunity to develop enhanced tuition and ensembles at no additional cost to the LEA. These changes were approved and the trust was granted charitable status in 1987. The County Council was the sole trustee of the Trust and a board was set up consisting of members of the education committee, education officers and co-opted parents. The trustees decide what they wish to purchase with the money raised from fees and grants and then pay the money over to the County Council, which makes purchases on the Trust's behalf. The Trust regularly pays £90,000 to the County Council for the employment of two FTE teachers and clerical assistants, rent of premises and miscellaneous items.

Current funding for the East Sussex Music Service

The music service now has three main elements: an LEA grant for the County Music School, the money raised by the County Music Trust, and a separate LEA expansion scheme for instrumental music in schools.

An LEA grant of £950,000 is used to pay for the original pre-1985 establishment, including area and county youth orchestras, bands and choirs. The Trust manages the music centres which now have a roll of 2,400 pupils who pay £20 a term membership fee.

The major new element is the revenue raised by the expansion scheme. Parents are charged £26.00 per term for their child's lessons in schools. Currently about 20 per cent of pupils receiving tuition are exempt from fees. (This compares with approximately 16 per cent of children receiving free school meals in the authority.) The new income has been used to employ 20 additional peripatetic staff, to offer promotion opportunities to staff and to purchase instruments. It has also enabled the service to develop (including commissioning new building work) and to offer an enhanced music INSET programme to teachers. Some of the money has been devoted to the administration of the parental fees system (for example, staffing and computer equipment).

The LEA grant to the music service helps fund concerts, courses and projects. The grant is supplemented by fees (for example, for summer courses), box office income and sponsorship to produce a turnover in excess of £80,000. The County has an active programme of schools' music festivals and concerts, involving thousands of children. East Sussex also organises its own schools' promenade concert each year.

The music projects enable schools to benefit from working with professional groups such as Opera 80, London Sinfonietta, the Composers Ensemble and the Brighton Jazz Cooperative. The courses are open to all young musicians in the area. Every year a summer school is held during the final weeks of the school term. This offers a wide choice of courses in such areas as music theatre, string playing, choral singing, recorders, percussion and orchestral playing.

Staffing and tuition

The East Sussex Music Service currently employs 63 instrumental teachers who teach mainly strings, woodwind and brass. There are two music advisers and a team of three advisory teachers who work in the primary and special schools, helping to support and develop classroom music. In addition there are three preparatory course tutors and a project coordinator, who organises the music projects.

East Sussex has 220 primary schools, 38 secondary schools and 20 special schools. The peripatetic service covers all primary and secondary schools in the authority. The special schools do not receive visits from the peripatetic staff. This is because there is a lack of expertise within the peripatetic staff to enable them to work effectively with children with special educational needs. On the other hand, teachers in special schools are offered INSET opportunities and much of the project work is centred on the special schools. For example, in a recent project a group of musicians from Glyndebourne worked with a number of schools for children with severe learning difficulties. The project took 'animals in danger' as its theme and involved the children in visiting Dudley Zoo.

Instrumental lessons take place in schools in school time. Pupils are withdrawn from lessons in small groups (a maximum of six per group for string players and four per group for other instruments). These lessons are termed 'master classes' and although they are group lessons, each child receives a significant element of individual tuition. This enables the service to charge parents for individual tuition within the legal framework of the legislation regarding charging for school activities.

East Sussex is keen to emphasise that the music service is now led by parent and pupil demand. The number of pupils receiving tuition has grown rapidly from 2,830 in 1989/90 to a projected level of 5,700 in 1991/92. The LEA believes that the service is open to any child who wishes to learn to play an instrument, rather than being targeted on the 'talented' few.

The service is also responsive to the needs of schools. In 1988 the primary heads' steering group challenged the LEA's decision to keep central funding for the music service rather than to devolve the money to schools. Members of the music service gave presentations to the heads about the current provision and plans to expand the service to all schools in the future. After the presentations the heads agreed not to seek devolution of the money for the service.

The service has since instituted a consultation process whereby all schools are visited three times a year by the heads of music centres, in addition to the in-service visits of the music advisory staff. In response to requests from the heads, the music service has devoted resources to: providing more advisory support for music in schools, such as advice on primary music and music technology; providing more live music in schools; purchasing a variety of instruments (especially large expensive items and 'non-Western' instruments) which are loaned to schools; expanding the provision of concerts and courses; and developing projects involving professional musicians working with schools.

Visiting schools regularly enables the service staff to identify and respond to needs of individual schools. The visits usually include observation of classroom music lessons and instrumental tuition. A meeting is held with the headteacher and the music coordinator. The aim of this meeting is to discuss how the input of the music service can be used to benefit all the pupils in the school. For example, the school may wish the students who receive instrumental tuition to play for the school in assembly. The representative from the music school could then offer to help staff plan such an assembly.

Two secondary schools are currently being helped by the music school to fund building improvements. In one school, space for making music has been extremely limited. The grant from the music school will enable soundproofed practice rooms to be built. Once the improvements have been made, music school staff will hold 'recruitment recitals' in the school to stimulate students' interest in taking instrumental music lessons.

Views from the schools

The LEA has recently surveyed heads and governors on the issue of further delegation of central budgets for the East Sussex Music School. There are 278 heads in East Sussex, of whom 84 per cent voted to keep the service centrally funded. In informal workshop sessions for 139 heads and governors, almost 60 per cent said they wished to retain central funding for the music service and, if delegated, a further 16 per cent would wish to contract back into the existing service.

One of the heads who would like to see the money delegated is David Pratt of Little Common Primary School in Bexhill. David Pratt says he is broadly very satisfied with the instrumental service: 'It is a high quality service with high quality people. It enhances what we as a school have to offer.' However, he would like the money to be delegated because 'we want to make our own decisions'. His main criticism of the way the service operates, centres around the withdrawal of children from lessons to receive instrumental tuition. His concern is that children regularly miss the same lessons. In the opinion of David Pratt and his governing body, music should be offered as an after school activity, open to any child who wishes to take part, but should not take place during the school day. David Pratt feels that the provision of music lessons in school time begs the question: 'Why are the top cricketers and top chess players not offered a similar service?' If delegated, he would like to buy back the music service 'but on our terms, we would want to buy in the music advisers and have the peripatetic staff visit during lunch time and after school'. David acknowledges that delegation of the music service budget would suit his large primary school, whereas his colleagues in smaller rural schools could lose because they would have difficulty in finding teachers willing to travel to their schools for small amounts of instrumental work.

At Thomas Peacocke Secondary School in Rye, Miss Lois Benton, the head of music, is also concerned about the timetabling of instrumental lessons. Although children are on a rota system, whereby the time of their instrumental lesson is different each week, the effect of the rota depends on the number of children learning a particular instrument: 'It has occurred that children felt their school work was suffering. For some instruments it is not such a problem but, for example, the oboe teacher only comes for an hour and a half so that is only three half-hour lessons. Children do regularly miss the same lesson. In order to prevent this affecting the work of older students, lessons are arranged during the lunch break or during the students' free periods.'

On the whole, Lois Benton is very satisfied with the service the school receives. The school has 26 hours' teaching time from seven teachers covering violin, viola, cello, double bass, brass, saxophone, flute, oboe and clarinet. Approximately 70 students out of the 850 in the school have some form of tuition. Lois Benton feels that the instrumental tuition enhances the work of the school: 'From the first year they (the pupils) bring their instruments and play in the classroom.' She also feels that it has given a 'tremendous impetus' to the performing element of the music GCSE course. Another benefit is that the school has been able to form four ensembles and bands as well as a school orchestra. The opening of a music centre in Hastings was a very welcome development, enabling children from Thomas Peacocke School to take part in ensembles and bands with children from other schools in the area.

Lois Benton initially greeted the introduction of charges for instrumental lessons with concern because the school serves 'an area of need'. However, the charging policy does not seem to have adversely affected the take up of tuition in the school. This is probably due to the remission scheme, although Lois does not know which children in the school receive free music tuition because this is handled by staff at the East Sussex Music School.

Looking to the future

Roger Durston believes that if in many LEAs the existing central funding for the music service is devolved to schools, 'it will deplete the service for everyone'. However, he is confident that, if devolution comes, the majority of heads in East Sussex will be keen to buy back the service, although in the short term some will use private teachers as cheaper alternatives.

The Croydon Music Teaching Agency

Introduction

Colin Evans is Director of the Croydon Music Teaching Agency (MTA). He has worked in Croydon for four years and was formerly a Music Coordinator for the ILEA. In 1988 he put forward a plan to transform the existing Croydon music support service into an agency. At that time, discussions were being held with schools about the likely devolution of central funds to schools under LMS. The Agency was set up in 1989 and now sells tuition to schools. Schools pay for this from their devolved budgets and in many cases, by charging parents. Since the Agency was established, instrumental tuition has expanded considerably due to schools buying additional hours of tuition.

Funding

When the Agency was formed in April 1989, the LEA budget of £300,000 for instrumental music was devolved to schools. The Agency currently receives funding from the LEA to support the senior management team and the central administration of the Agency. The funding for 'Community Activities' ie music centres, choirs and orchestras, was not devolved to schools. Colin Evans would prefer to keep these as centrally funded items because he feels that it would be difficult to recoup costs under a formula funding arrangement. Despite the fact that Community Activities are paid for from the education budget whereas tuition is paid for by schools, these activities are all managed by the MTA.

It has been proposed that the funding for management and administration could be wholly or partly devolved to schools in future. If this does happen, the Agency would have to recoup the money by either increasing its charges to schools or offering schools 'service contracts' which would guarantee certain levels of service.

At present, schools are charged a flat fee of £15.90 for an hour's tuition. This includes the cost of National Insurance, and travel. However, employment costs vary considerably from about £13 an hour for part-time instructors to about £25 per hour for full-time staff. In future, the Agency may charge differentiated fees according to the qualifications and experience of the teacher.

When the Agency was set up and it was decided to delegate the central funding, each school's current level of provision was taken into account as well as the number of pupils in the school. This arrangement was a temporary measure in order to ease the transition to full 'formula' funding (ie an allocation based entirely on pupil numbers) over a period of three years. Colin Evans commented that several small schools which had generous allocations of instrumental time under the previous system have maintained their previous level of provision by setting up charging policies.

Schools pay for tuition from their delegated budgets. Some schools, particularly those in the more affluent south of the borough, charge parents for individual or small group tuition. Fees vary from around £1.00 to £8.00 for a 30-minute lesson. A number of the schools which charge parents have remission schemes for children whose parents cannot afford to pay. Colin Evans commented that the fact that schools charge parents at different rates (while some do not charge at all) shows that: 'schools know their parents and are aware of what parents can afford to pay'. The introduction of parental charging has supported the expansion of the Agency's staffing from 33.5 FTE teaching staff in 1989/90 to 42.9 FTE staff in 1991/92.

Staffing and tuition

The Music Teaching Agency is managed by a senior management team comprising Colin Evans and three Area Music Coordinators. Although the Area Music Coordinators have a line management role within their instrumental specialism, their key function is to liaise with and support schools in the development of their instrumental programmes. The Agency currently employs 125 music teachers/instructors of whom 112 work part-time. There are also two clerical staff who help run the Agency.

The Agency currently provides a music service to nearly all of Croydon's primary and secondary schools. (One school has not engaged the service, preferring to buy in cheaper private tutors.) Two of the six special schools also use in the service, and more may do so next term. These special schools are currently looking at ways of developing instrumental music, using a small central budget set aside for this purpose.

Responding to demand

Before LMS, the music service provided tuition for all the primary and secondary schools in Croydon. The pattern of provision was, however, based on historical precedent rather than on the number of children in the school. This meant that some heads were reluctant to review the needs of the school, in case their hours were subsequently reduced. Colin Evans argues that, under LMS, the Agency is able to meet school needs more effectively than the previous service could, because schools pay for the service, and negotiate provision to meet their needs. Because of the financial implications, Colin feels that schools take much greater care in planning their instrumental programmes, and in assessment and reporting.

In the term before the Agency came into being, Colin Evans visited nearly every school in Croydon to discuss the situation with the headteachers. This was a very time-consuming exercise, but Colin believes that it was vital to the Agency's success. He was able to discuss with each headteacher the needs of the school and to identify new areas of demand for music support.

Although most primary and secondary schools had been receiving some tuition from the music service, the majority of the 30 infant schools had not received any instrumental tuition. When the Agency was being devised, Colin discussed with the infant school heads what kind of provision they would like to purchase in future from their delegated funds. There were two main areas of demand: support for classroom music and instrumental tuition tailored for young children. In response to this, the Agency has recruited 10 part-time music teachers to work in infant classes helping the schools to prepare for the introduction of music as a foundation subject in the National Curriculum. Three infant schools now have visits from instrumental teachers who specialise in Suzuki-style violin tuition which is reported to be running very successfully and has the active support of parents.

Marketing the Agency

The initial visits to all headteachers in Croydon formed the basis of the Agency's marketing approach. This has since been followed up by a series of LMS Guidelines, a detailed paper on instrumental assessment and a regular newsletter to headteachers.

Agency staff are in the process of producing a booklet aimed at parents. This booklet will outline the range of services on offer (for example, tuition, instrument purchase, music centre activities) and stress the high quality of tuition provided by the Agency. The

Agency also enables schools to have a member of the MTA staff present at parents' evenings, to talk to parents about the advantages of instrumental tuition for their children.

The MTA has three quintets which give performances in schools. Since the establishment of the Agency, the work of the quintets was reviewed. Now, rather than give one-off performances, the MTA sends a teachers' pack to schools before the visit. The pack contains tapes of the quintets' repertoire and guidance on some simple activities which teachers can use with their classes in preparation for the musicians' performance. These visits are seen by the Agency as providing an excellent opportunity to market its services to teachers and pupils.

Future plans

Colin Evans is cautiously optimistic about the future for the Croydon Music Teaching Agency. He feels that a great deal has already been achieved and that schools and parents are taking instrumental music much more seriously than previously: 'Schools are much more careful to monitor the quality and appropriateness of the provision and take a more active interest in the appointment of instrumental teachers to the school'. MTA staff have also become involved to a greater extent in classroom activities, helping teachers to develop their music curriculum and assisting in the assessment of students for GCSE. This type of activity will expand when music is introduced into the National Curriculum.

In order to respond to demand for introductory lessons, the MTA is considering setting up out-of-school tuition centres which will charge parents for their child's tuition. However, Colin feels that it is essential to preserve the main link with classroom music by offering the majority of tuition in school time. Colin himself exemplifies this link between instrumental tuition and classroom music, by dividing his time equally between his post as Director of the MTA and his work in an advisory capacity for Croydon LEA.

Advice to others

Colin Evans has received many phone calls and visits from colleagues in other LEAs wishing to explore the possibilities of setting up music agencies themselves. However, he is cautious about how far the Croydon model would work in other authorities. His advice is that those in charge of music services should have a detailed grasp of the financial situation of their service and its current market. 'Unless you know the total school population, the number of children learning instruments, the cost for teachers and administration, as well as the total amount of money available, it's very difficult to make any plans, let alone justify keeping money if you don't know how much is there.' He also feels that a great deal of planning and consultation with headteachers is required before any change is implemented. Colin believes that delegation of the money to schools may help preserve these services in future because retained central funding can be vulnerable. He feels that some LEAs might find it extremely difficult to raise additional money from parental contributions, and suggests that it might be useful for these LEAs to reconsider the type of provision they offer. Instrumental tuition is costly to provide, especially when taking account of the cost of musical instruments. It may be necessary for some LEAs to devise a completely new approach to their instrumental teaching, for example class-based music workshops or heterogenous instrumental tuition grouping (which is a common form of grouping for instrumental tuition in the USA). Colin Evans predicted that in future: 'Certainly the war-cry "Instrumental Music for All" will need to be re-examined'.

The Foundation For Young Musicians

Introduction

Chris Crowcroft is a consultant on arts and public affairs sponsorship. He first became involved in advising on sponsorship for instrumental music when he was asked to carry out a feasibility study to look at the future of instrumental tuition in central London after the abolition of the ILEA. It was on the basis of this study that the Foundation for Young Musicians (FYM) was set up in 1990.

Chris has maintained an interest in instrumental work, and is currently acting as a consultant to two LEAs, advising them on the marketing and sponsorship possibilities for instrumental music in their areas.

Establishing the Foundation and Centre for Young Musicians

When the abolition of the ILEA was announced, there was a groundswell of concern about the future of centrally organised instrumental music tuition in inner London. The Government reacted to this concern by commissioning a feasibility study to explore the possibility of plural funding to support a foundation for young musicians. The funding was to come from a combination of central government, local government, parents, commercial sponsors and grant-making trusts.

Chris Crowcroft took an early view that such a Foundation could not, itself, take over the funding of all the ILEA music tuition. A two-tier system was proposed: the Foundation was to take on the funding of a variety of bands, ensembles and orchestras, including the London Schools Symphony Orchestra (LSSO). It was also to be responsible for the costs of central organising staff and their overheads, and extra costs such as the formation of a music library and supplementing the instrument collection. Instrumental tuition in schools would be the responsibility of the new London authorities. They would also pay the direct tuition costs of children from their areas who attended a music centre serving all the inner London authorities. Chris Crowcroft proposed to extend the scope of the new Foundation to build up the programme of the LSSO and to establish a series of master classes for students.

As part of the feasibility study, Chris spoke to representatives from the proposed new inner London authorities and sounded out potential sponsors. From the local government representatives, he gained a commitment to the principle of per capita funding up to a ceiling representing 50 per cent of the true cost of tuition. Westminster had agreed to act as 'lead borough' for the Foundation, maintaining the music centre (known as the Centre for Young Musicians or CYM) in its area, with a second centre operating from Mile End. Authorities agreed to pay between £250 and £1,000 per pupil per year. It was suggested that the top rate for each pupil should be just under £1,000 because it was difficult to get councils to vote through sums of £1,000 or more.

Approaches to potential commercial sponsors and charitable trusts revealed that there would be considerable support for the new Foundation, provided that it was seen to be developmental and to enjoy government support. Some sponsors wanted their funding to go into special projects which would lend prestige to the name of the sponsor. A minority were willing for their money to go into less high profile areas, such as general costs. A few of the sponsors approached at this stage said they were somewhat reluctant to support the new Foundation, believing that they should not be asked to support something which should be paid for from the public purse. Such 'government backfill' is a controversial area for some funding bodies, particularly in the area of arts sponsorship.

Funding and Operation of the Foundation for Young Musicians

The Foundation for Young Musicians is supported by what Chris Crowcroft describes as 'mixed economy' funding. All the main funding 'partners' have made a commitment to the Foundation for a three-year period. Chris believes that this is an optimal length of time as far as sponsors are concerned. (Few sponsors wish to commit themselves beyond three years).

The Department of Education and Science has agreed to contribute a minimum of £100,000 a year to funding the Foundation. This represents approximately 80 per cent of the central staffing costs for the CYM. The LEA money covers the cost of tuition only.

The majority of sponsors were each asked to commit an annual amount of £10,000 to the Foundation. Most of the current sponsors are Charitable Foundations which give support to the arts or for young people. The Foundation for Young Musicians has also attracted large and small-scale sponsorship for specific projects such as the acquisition of instruments, the music library, and a series of recitals and master classes. Because of the amounts of money involved, Chris Crowcroft suggested approaching large national companies with a local investment in London. The support of London Electricity for the London Schools Symphony Orchestra is an example of the success of this strategy. This grant is worth £50,000 a year and is augmented by a government grant from the Business Sponsorship Incentive Scheme.

As well as these funding bodies, the Foundation has asked parents to contribute through covenants. The aim was to raise £10,000 a year from parents, and now one in three parents contribute an average of £8.00 a month in this way. The feasibility study showed that simply charging a fee to parents would not be workable or desirable. This was because some parents would be unable or unwilling to pay. It was also an unacceptable proposition for some of the new local authorities, which disagreed with the principle of levying charges for a previously free service. Chris commented that it was very important to raise money from parents through covenants, because it showed their commitment to the Foundation and this, in turn, encouraged other outside sponsors to become partners in the initiative.

On Chris Crowcroft's advice, the Foundation for Young Musicians is both a charity and a limited company. This dual status has several advantages: charitable status enables the Foundation to attract donations and receive money from covenants in a tax-efficient form. The fact that the Foundation is also a limited company protects the position of the trustees (who are also the company directors). In the event of financial loss, the trustees would not be held financially liable for the Foundation's debts.

The Foundation's main role is to raise funds to meet the core costs for the operation of the CYM. There is a deliberate separation between the role of the trustees and that of the Director of the CYM. The trustees' role is to raise money in a three-year rolling programme. The main responsibility for the policy and operation of the CYM lies with its Director, Peter Shave. He reports to a management committee and ultimately to a Policy Executive Committee which represents all interested groups: local authorities, parents, students, teachers and the Foundation.

Chris Crowcroft reported that the CYM is now running successfully. It employs a central team of 17 tutors who oversee term-time tuition and run a variety of holiday courses for children in both Western classical and 'non-Western' music-making, for around 600 children per year. The instrument collection and music library are being built up, and the work of the London Schools Symphony Orchestra has expanded into an impressive concert programme held in many large venues (e.g. open air concerts at Kenwood House). Many of these concerts can be attended by London school children free of charge. New pieces have been commissioned for the orchestra, and the young musicians have benefited from working with some of the country's top conductors, including Jane Glover, Simon Rattle and Sir Michael Tippett.

Looking to the future

Chris Crowcroft hopes that the Foundation for Young Musicians will continue to prosper in future. But its position is dependent on the continuation of government, as well as other funding, and the goodwill of parents and the inner London authorities in particular.

The Trustees will have to work hard at fund raising to keep some of their current sponsors after the first three years of operation and to attract new ones. They are also dependent on Westminster continuing to act as lead borough (and to allow them use of the CYM building) and the 12 other authorities' willingness to pay for the young people from their areas who attend. Chris stresses that there is no one-off solution to this kind of fund raising and that the FYM will require constant work from all the 'partners' in the enterprise (particularly the parents, trustees and organisers) to keep it going in future.

Advice to others

Chris Crowcroft does not believe that the FYM 'model' would automatically work if implemented in other areas. Yet he can identify some principles which he believes might form useful guidance for others facing an uncertain future for their instrumental music services.

1. Chris suggests that the first step for any music service should be to test the political support for continued local government funding of a music service. This is best done by 'galvanising parents into action'. Parents can prove useful allies, especially

if local politicians need to be convinced of the arguments in favour of subsidising instrumental tuition. A group of parents is also likely to have many contacts which could be useful in mounting such a campaign. Chris advises that the main aim should be to fight for the continued existence of the service, paid for by the local authority. However, he believes that campaign organisers should have a second plan which would enable a small central team to be retained if local government funding is reduced or cut altogether.

2. The second principle is to tailor the arguments in favour of the service, to the audience being addressed. In some cases this may mean highlighting the prestige conveyed on the area by a youth choir or orchestra; in others, it may mean pointing out the support of the service for class music, or its success in meeting the needs of children from disadvantaged backgrounds.

3. Chris feels that those involved in the running of music services need to make a well-researched and professionally presented case for funding. If music services can gain the support of local parents and reasonable financial commitment from local government, then other sponsors may consider putting in funding too. (It is Chris Crowcroft's experience that, without such local support, especially from local government, other sponsors will be wary of contributing to keeping a service going.)

4. In some ways the total 'privatisation' of instrumental services is the most difficult option. This means creating a new enterprise almost from scratch and is only really viable where some financial support (e.g. a local business grant) is available to help underwrite the new enterprise. In Chris's view, outside sponsorship can only ever be part of the picture, never a total replacement of costs.

Looking to the future

Chris does not believe that, in the absence of political will, it would be possible to keep instrumental services operating in all areas of the country. If there is not enough support for the service in a locality, and little hope of raising money through parental contributions or local business sponsorship, then the continuation of the service is in the hands of the local authority. If such local authorities are hit by financial cutbacks, and fail to protect the instrumental service, then it is quite likely that some areas will lose their instrumental provision altogether unless a form of central government funding (such as the DES grant to the FYM) were to be made more widely available.

Postscript

After this interview was carried out, there was a press report (*Education,* 1991) that pupils attending the CYM had been warned of a possible reduction in the length of their lessons. This was attributed to funding constraints caused by the 'severe financial difficulties being experienced by some London boroughs'.

The Knowsley Instrumental Music Service

Introduction

In Knowsley, the instrumental music service forms part of the Performing Arts Team. Paul Morris, Adviser for the Performing Arts, has worked for Knowsley for 17 years. At the time of this study Paul was ending his career in Knowsley, taking early retirement from the Authority. Steve Titchmarsh is Head of Performing Arts. He joined the Authority two years ago from Cheshire LEA. The Performing Arts Team was formed a few years ago and its core members are the staff of the former peripatetic music service, together with a dance/music coordinator and a drama coordinator. Paul Morris supported the establishment of the performing arts team and the creation of a new post for the head of the team.

In 1989/90 instrumental teachers visited the majority of the 68 primary and 11 secondary schools, providing tuition for about 10 per cent of the primary and secondary population. The four music centres were attended by 600 pupils, mainly from the primary sector. Knowsley is a small authority with problems of social deprivation, yet it has an impressive range of musical activity, from involvement in class music, and residencies with groups of professional musicians to a youth concert band, a jazz orchestra, two youth orchestras and two youth choirs.

At the time of my visit to Knowsley there were some uncertainties about the future of the instrumental support service. Some reduction in funding had been effected, and possibilities were being explored of further devolution of central funding to schools. Staff were understandably concerned about their future, and some had shown an increased level of interest in alternative employment.

Funding for the instrumental support service

Up to now, the instrumental support service has been funded centrally by the LEA. Tuition is provided free and there is a stock of instruments on loan to parents and schools. Parents are encouraged to buy an instrument for their child after one year of tuition but many cannot afford to do so. In such cases, the LEA continues to provide instruments for the child's use. The LEA also currently pays for major instrument repairs, equipment and sheet music.

In 1990, Knowsley Council was faced with the need to make substantial reductions in the education budget. A policy decision was made to keep cuts in schools budgets as small as possible. This inevitably meant that centrally funded services, such as the instrumental support service had a larger reduction in budgets. The budget for the complete Performing Arts Team was set at £217,000 for 1990/91, a cut of 25 per cent on the previous year's budget.

Paul Morris had responsibility for organising the service with this reduced budget. Schools now receive somewhat less peripatetic support than in the past, and the size of some tuition groups has been increased. Some economies have been made by adjusting the arrangements for Knowsley Choir and Orchestra rehearsals.

The effect of Local Management of Schools

Much greater care is now being taken to apportion the services of the team equitably between schools. A pilot scheme is being operated by which schools can 'buy in' additional support from the team. Not unnaturally schools which 'buy in' members of the team feel they have a right to specify the precise activities in which such members will engage. This has led to some situations in which what team members themselves would like to do is different from what the schools require.

View from the schools

Three headteachers gave views about the service. (They are not necessarily representative of opinions across the whole Authority.) Peter Barlow is head of Prescot Secondary School which had 760 pupils in 1990/91. Gill Lucy and Frank Ravey are primary headteachers. Frank Ravey's school, St. Aidans, had 232 pupils and Gill Lucy's school, Mosscroft Primary, had 300 full-time pupils and 52 part-time nursery places.

All these schools currently receive some tuition from the peripatetic staff. Two years ago, when Gill Lucy took up her headship, Mosscroft was receiving no instrumental tuition. Gill contacted Steve Titchmarsh to find out why this was so, and discovered that the previous head had not particularly encouraged music in the school. She asked for the school to be put on the timetable for peripatetic visits and now two teachers visit her school for an hour's tuition each week.

Until recently, Prescot Secondary School received 13 hours' tuition a week. When the service was redistributed last year, the amount of tuition at Prescot was cut to four hours. Mr. Barlow described his school as having a good reputation for music and actively supporting a school orchestra. He said that the cutbacks in instrumental tuition had caused considerable difficulties for the school. When the instrumental music budget is devolved to schools, Mr. Barlow intends to buy back 12 hours a week, asking parents to contribute to the cost of lessons. (Although a survey of parents revealed a demand in the school for about 16 hours' tuition, this has proved too great an expense for the school governors to underwrite.)

All three heads reported that demand for tuition from parents and pupils usually exceeds supply. This means that the schools must select the children who receive tuition. In the secondary schools, priority is given to those already learning an instrument when they join the school. Other children are put on a waiting list until places become available. The two primary schools select children in consultation with peripatetic teachers. Gill Lucy said that she now has a constant stream of requests from parents who would like their children to receive tuition. Despite her personal support for music, she finds it difficult to deal with these requests: 'Quite frankly it would be a lot easier not to have it at all. I'm creating a monster now and I don't think I can cope with the demand.' In addition to the two hours' tuition per week, Mosscroft School has recently received some help from the service in the form of classroom support. Gill has used INSET funds to pay for a member of the Performing Arts Team to work with teachers and their classes. (Such income for the team has been used to mitigate the full effects of the central budget cuts.)

All three heads have considered the possibility of raising money from parents. In the case of Prescot School, school staff have made 'discreet enquiries' among parents about the possibility of introducing charges for tuition at around £36 per term. Peter Barlow commented that this suggestion has led some parents to seek private tuition, 'because they know they can get it cheaper'. He is concerned that this will affect the quality of instrumental music in the school.

Gill Lucy has considered asking parents to pay a small amount (around 50p per week) towards the cost of instrument repair, which could become the responsibility of the schools in future. But she is not hopeful of raising even this small amount: 'We have horrendous problems getting 50p a term milk money!' Frank Ravey points out that his school is the sixth most deprived in the Borough: 'I couldn't countenance asking people without two halfpennies to rub together to pay for music!' He is concerned about the cost of instrument repairs: 'Even a small repair costs seventy pounds. Then what you do is put it in a cupboard and forget about it.'

These three heads are committed to continuing to offer some form of instrumental tuition in future, but they acknowledge that some of their colleagues are unlikely to do so.

Looking to the future

Although some pessimistic views about the future of the service have been expressed in recent months, there are reported to be positive aspects of the changes taking place. If schools move to a situation where they 'buy in' the services of the team, a far more effective spirit of partnership may evolve. Brian Lord, Senior Assistant Director of Knowsley LEA, explained: 'Early indications are that schools will buy in the services of the team on a fairly large scale. It is possible that the "buying process" will, in due course, generate a larger team than the existing one.'

Constraints and opportunities: a summary

Music agencies, trusts and foundations can seem to be an attractive alternative to music services run by an LEA, particularly at a time of such uncertainty for music service staff. Yet there are also a number of potential disadvantages and constraints which affect the operation of such semi-autonomous organisations. The main constraints and opportunities affecting music trusts, agencies and foundations are given below. Some of the points are drawn from papers presented at a recent conference held by the UK Council for Music Education and Training (Durston, R. 1991, and Willis, K. 1991) and some from the experiences of those contributing to this research.

CONSTRAINTS AFFECTING MUSIC AGENCIES, TRUSTS AND FOUNDATIONS

1. A music agency or trust may not be viable in some areas, particularly where many parents are unable to pay for tuition.

2. Most agencies and trusts rely on generating money from parents. Many people are strongly opposed to the principle of charging for an educational service such as instrumental tuition.

3. It may not be legal to set up an agency or trust principally to enable fees to be charged for tuition, because this could be seen as an attempt to circumvent the law on charging for school activities.

4. Although remission schemes, bursaries and subsidies help support children of parents who cannot afford to pay, such schemes are not always able to cope with demand. Charging policies may discourage some parents from requesting tuition for their child.

5. There are considerable costs in setting up administration schemes for collecting fees and operating a payroll. There has to be some procedure for dealing with bad debts. It is possible that services provided by music agencies may be liable for Value Added Tax.

6. Teaching staff may have less job security and poorer conditions of employment than those employed by an LEA service. For example, there may be an increase in self-employment and part-time work in place of full-time employment. Staff may be required to work longer hours, to teach more children and may not have access to LEA probationary or pension schemes.

7. An agency or trust will not necessarily have as close a relationship with music advisers/inspectors as an LEA service. This could make it difficult for LEAs to coordinate the contribution of the instrumental music service to the music curriculum in schools.

8. It can take up to two years to set up a music trust. An application for charitable status will take several months to process.

OPPORTUNITIES PROVIDED BY AGENCIES, TRUSTS AND FOUNDATIONS

1.   If LEAs or local government are reorganised, a trust or agency could continue to offer a tuition service to schools and parents.

2.   Trusts can receive money from non-education budgets, which makes them less vulnerable to cuts (caused, for example, by community charge capping, LMS or schools opting out of LEA control).

3.   Because it is a third party, a trust or agency may levy charges for tuition in circumstances where an LEA or school cannot.

4.   A music trust or foundation can apply for charitable status. This allows for parents to give money in the form of covenants. It may also attract sponsors who will make donations to charities but would not be willing to contribute towards an LEA service.

5.   Agencies/trusts can be more responsive to demand than an LEA service. This could allow the instrumental service to expand and diversify into other 'markets'.

6.   Many LEA services operate a selection policy, based on an assessment of a pupil's musical ability. An agency or trust which charges parents for tuition has to be responsive to parent demand. Thus, it is argued that under an agency or trust, the service is effectively broadened to allow access to pupils with a wider range of musical abilities.

7.   An agency or trust is perhaps more likely than a service to use marketing strategies. This should enable it to achieve a high profile for the instrumental music service within the authority.

Conclusion

This study has revealed that staffing levels for the instrumental service as a whole are estimated to be at about the same level as in 1986, and that the overall level of provision to schools and pupils is estimated to have risen since the 1986 survey. Does this mean that the fears expressed for the future of instrumental services by music educators, musicians and parents are therefore unfounded?

The picture emerging from the evidence presented in this research is a complex one. First, it appears that both staffing and provision have risen after the first survey, but have declined more recently. (This is illustrated by the five per cent overall drop in staffing reported by 82 LEAs since 1989).

Second, some areas have undoubtedly suffered greater cutbacks than others, and two authorities have cut their instrumental music services entirely since 1990. This is obviously a worrying development which has caused considerable concern. In the absence of funding from central government funding, it is possible that other services may be forced to close in future.

Third, although over a third of LEAs reported funding cuts between 1989/90 and 1990/91, a small minority reported increases in funding in the same period. Therefore funding cuts have not been distributed equally among LEAs.

Last, it is evident that some people are looking into the future, when they believe that a number of potentially worrying changes are likely to take place. Chief amongst these is the pressure on authorities to delegate centrally held funding to schools. This eventuality was greeted with concern by about a third of respondents, who felt that it would have a largely negative effect on their services.

Clearly, then, the fears for the future of instrumental music services in some areas of the country were based in reality. It is certainly disheartening for the music service staff in these areas, who feel they have achieved so much over the years, to be faced with cutting back their service. This is taking place at the time when the service could play a major role in supporting the introduction of the new National Curriculum for music throughout England and Wales.

It was not the intention of this study to provide a set of recommendations for future practice. Many of the recommendations contained in the previous NFER report *A Sound Start* are just as relevant for the 1990s, and it is not helpful to offer extensive suggestions for future action to those facing stringent financial cutbacks. However, many service managers still have room for manoeuvre, and it is hoped that the following list of questions will prove useful to them in reviewing their current practice and in making plans for the future.

SOME SUGGESTED ACTION POINTS FOR THE MANAGERS OF INSTRUMENTAL MUSIC SERVICES

Service managers may find it helpful to work with their staff in order to identify the potential threats and opportunities which are likely to affect the operation of their services in future.

Once identified, these threats and opportunities need to be examined closely in order to see what action staff could take to minimise the effects of the threats and to maximise the opportunities. An illustration of such a process, based on the findings of this research, is given below. However, it is recommended that each service should carry out their own analysis, since staff in each area will know of local circumstances which could affect the outcome of the review.

Threats posed to the instrumental music service

- Cuts in funding for the service caused by reductions in local government funding.

- Delegation of central funding to schools - heads and governors may buy back into the service at a lower level than that represented by the previous LEA funding.

- Threats to the continued existence of LEAs. If many schools 'opt out' of LEA control, they will take some of the central LEA funding with them.

- Possible 'low profile' of service in the authority - do many people really know what the music service is and what it does?

- Competition from other music tuition providers, such as students and private teachers.

Opportunities

- Local Management of Schools may mean some schools buying more tuition than they previously received, thus causing an increase in funding.

- The introduction of National Curriculum music is likely to increase demand for music support, especially in the primary sector.

- Other potential sources of funding could be exploited.

ACTION POINTS
FOR INSTRUMENTAL MUSIC STAFF

These points raise questions which are designed to provide a checklist for instrumental music staff. It is hoped that they will assist staff to determine how well their current arrangements are working and how far these might need to be adapted to meet future demands.

Know your service

● Decisions on the future of the service need to be based on fact. It is also important to show current and potential funders that the service is run efficiently.

● How many full-and part-time teachers does the service employ?

● What qualifications and experience do they have? How could this best be used and improved?

● How many pupils are taught in how many schools?

● Are staff deployed in the most cost-effective way?

● Would serving 'clusters' of schools be a useful method of targeting provision on more schools (particularly in rura areas)?

● How much does it cost to provide the service? What proportion of total costs is represented by such items as administration, overheads, travel, etc?

Exploit the possibilities

There are potential 'clients' who many services do not reach, yet who would be interested in receiving tuition/ support and who may, in future, be able to pay for it from their own budgets.

- Many services do not currently offer tuition in special schools. Is there a case for employing someone with this brief, who could also coordinate work for children with special educational needs in mainstream schools?

- Could the service serve other new clients such as young children (both pre-school age and those in infant schools), and adults (particularly those whose children are already receiving tuition)?

- Could the service exploit its resources in new ways, such as enabling schools, youth groups and others to use its expertise, instruments and premises? If so, would it be viable to charge a fee for, say, the use of recording equipment in a music centre?

- How could the service best meet the needs of class teachers for support in introducing National Curriculum music? For example, could instrumental music service staff run in-service training for school staff?

Capitalise on strengths

Many respondents to the survey said that they aimed to provide a high-quality service to schools and pupils. Centrally-run services have two main advantages over private tutors. First, they are large enough and should be flexible enough to cater for a variety of needs. Second, they should be able to guarantee a high standard of service.

- How flexible and efficient is the service in meeting requests from parents and/or schools?

- What methods are in place for monitoring the quality of the service? How could these be improved?

- Are schools, parents and pupils ever asked for their views?

- What action is necessary to improve the quality of the service in future?

Orchestrate support

In order to retain local authority support in a time of financial hardship, instrumental music services must mobilise existing support and raise awareness about the contribution of their services to the local community. Parents are an important source of potential support.

- Could the service do more to involve parents? If so, how?

- Are heads and governors convinced of the advantages of receiving/buying instrumental tuition from the service? If not, how could they be informed of its advantages for their school?

- Does the local community know of the existence of the service and value what the service has to offer?

- How much publicity does the service get in the local press? How could this be developed?

- Are local councillors involved? If not, how could service staff and parents best convince them of the value of their support?

- How much pressure could be brought to bear if the local authority threatened to withdraw funding for instrumental music?

> ## Explore other funding/organisational possibilities
>
> This report has contained some detailed information on the operation of music trusts and agencies. It is suggested that all LEA service managers should weigh up the potential advantages and disadvantages of these alternatives to an LEA service in their particular area. It should be noted that not all such alternatives involve charging parents for tuition (which is a particularly sensitive issue), and that it is possible to provide an LEA-funded instrumental service alongside a semi-autonomous agency or trust.
>
> ● Would the formation of an agency, trust or foundation enable the music service currently offered to be retained and/or to expand in future?

As John Stephens pointed out in his foreword to this book, music educators are currently experiencing a period of rapid change. Instrumental services have a record of which to be proud. Despite the recent fears for the service, there is much that service staff can (and should) do to ensure that in future, and for all pupils who could benefit, the music will play on.

References

ABRAMS, F. (1990). 'Cuts policies meet chorus of disapproval', *Times Educational Supplement,* 3886, 21 December, 3.

ADDISON, R. (1990). 'Parents' views on their children's musical education in the primary school: a survey', *British Journal of Music Education,* 7,2, July 1990, 133-41.

ASSOCIATION OF BRITISH ORCHESTRAS (1991). *LEA Lessons for Orchestral Players: Results of Survey Conducted by ABO Education Officers.*

CALOUSTE GULBENKIAN FOUNDATION (1978). *Training Musicians.* London: Calouste Gulbenkian Foundation.

CLEAVE, S. and DUST, K. (1989). *A Sound Start: The Schools' Instrumental Music Service.* Windsor: NFER-NELSON.

DURSTON, R. (1991). *'Address to UKCMET'.* Paper presented to the UK Council for Music Education and Training (UKMET) Conference, July. Huddersfield Polytechnic.

EDUCATION (1991). 'Last London centre faces the pinch', *Education,* 178, 14, 4 October, 267.

GREAT BRITAIN. DEPARTMENT OF EDUCATION AND SCIENCE. HER MAJESTY'S INSPECTORATE (1985). *Music from 5 to 16.* (Curriculum Matters 4) London: DES.

GREAT BRITAIN. DEPARTMENT OF EDUCATION AND SCIENCE (1989). *The Education Reform Act 1988: Charges for School Activities.* (Circular No. 2/89) London: DES.

GREAT BRITAIN. DEPARTMENT OF EDUCATION AND SCIENCE. HER MAJESTY'S INSPECTORATE (1991a). *Aspects Of Primary Education: The Teaching and Learning of Music*. London: HMSO.

GREAT BRITAIN. DEPARTMENT OF EDUCATION AND SCIENCE AND WELSH OFFICE (1991b). *Music for Ages 5 to 14: Proposals of the Secretary of State for Education and Science and the Secretary of State for Wales*. York: NCC.

GREAT BRITAIN. DEPARTMENT OF EDUCATION AND SCIENCE (1991c). *School Teacher Appraisal*. (Circular 12/91) London: DES.

GREAT BRITAIN. DEPARTMENT OF EDUCATION AND SCIENCE (1991d). *The Parents' Charter*. London: DES.

GREAT BRITAIN. PARLIAMENT. HOUSE OF LORDS (1991). Parliamentary debates (Hansard). Session 1990-1991. 'Musical instruments and theatre in schools.' Vol 526. 13 February 1991. Cols. 183-208. London: HMSO.

IZBICKI, J. (1981). 'Piper's paymaster lament', *Daily Telegraph*, 2 March, 11.

MACLEOD, D. (1991). 'Music at risk of playing second fiddle', *The Independent*, 31 January, 19.

MAYCHELL, K., KEYS, W. and STEEPLES, B. (1991). *Charging for School Activities*. Slough: NFER.

MILLS, J. (1985). 'Gifted instrumentalists: how can we recognise them?', *British Journal of Music Education*, 2,1, March, 39-49.

MUSICIANS UNION (1991). 'Cuts in instrumental teaching'. London: Musicians Union.

PYKE, N. (1991). 'Minister lambasts "appalling authorities"', *Times Educational Supplement*, 3919, 9 August, 4.

SHARP, C. and DUST, K. (1990). *Artists in Schools: A Handbook for Teachers and Artists*. London: Bedford Square Press.

WEINBERG, G. (1985). *The Secrets of Consulting: A Guide to Giving and Getting Advice Successfully*. New York: Dorset House Publishing.

WILLIS, K. (1991). 'The organisation of instrumental teaching'. Paper presented to the UK Council for Music Education and Training (UKCMET) Conference, July 1991. Huddersfield Polytechnic.

Related publications

CLEAVE, S. and SHARP, C. (1986). *The Arts: A Preparation to Teach.* Slough: NFER.

CLEAVE, S. and DUST, K. (1989). *A Sound Start: The Schools' Instrumental Music Service.* Windsor: NFER-Nelson.

MAYCHELL, K. *et al* (1991). *Charging for School Activities.* Slough: NFER.

SHARP, C. and DUST, K. (1990). *Artists in Schools: A Handbook for Teachers and Artists.* London: Bedford Square Press.

SHARP, C. (1990). *Developing the Arts in Primary Schools: Good Practice in Teacher Education.* Slough: NFER.

SHARP, C. (1991). *Performing Arts Education 16-19, Towards Good Practice.* (Conference Report) Cambridge: Eastern Arts Association.

Other publications

Other in-house publications available from the NFER include:

The Work and Impact of Advisory Teachers

The Changing Role, Structure and Style of LEAs

About Change: Schools' and LEAs' Perspectives on   LEA Reorganization

Enabling Teachers to Undertake INSET

A Survey of School Governing Bodies

Towards Effective Partnerships in School Governance

Foreign Languages for Lower Attaining Pupils

Staff Appraisal: The FE Pilot Schemes

Research into Engineering Education

Education: Guide to European Organizations and Programmes

Register of Research in Special Education, Vol 2

Four Year Olds in School: Quality Matters

Vocational Education Opportunities for Students with Speech and Language Impairments

SACREs: Their Formation, Composition, Operation and Role on RE and Worship

Multi-Agency Support for Special Needs

The Impact of School-Focused INSET on Classroom Practice

The Impact of INSET: The Case of Primary Science

Re-Organizing Post-16 Education: The Tertiary Option

Copies of these publications are obtainable from:

Dissemination Unit, NFER, The Mere, Upton Park, SLOUGH, SL1 2DQ